"Each friend represents a world in us, a world possibly not born until they arrive."

Happy Birthday – sometime this week

VWO.

Social Work and Innovation

An Anthology of Advanced Level Practice

Edited by
Stan Houston, Vivian McConvey,
Marian O'Rourke and Marcella Leonard

Central Council for Education and Training in Social Work

Published by Central Council for Education and Training in Social Work
Derbyshire House, St Chad's Street, London WC1H 8AD

Produced by CCETSW (NI)
6 Malone Road, Belfast BT9 5BN

First published January 2001

ISBN 1 85719 224 9

Designed and typeset by Radian Design 028 9754 1506
Cover designed by Jane McBeigh 028 9058 4151
Printed by GPS Colour Graphics Ltd 028 9070 2020

CONTENTS

CONTRIBUTORS

Stan Houston is a lecturer in social work at Queen's University, Belfast. Before this he worked as a practitioner, trainer and manager in children's services in the eastern area of Northern Ireland. He is interested in theorising social work and co-ordinates the MSc in advanced social work with colleagues from the University of Ulster.

Billy McCullough is a lecturer in social work at the University of Ulster at Jordanstown. He has carried out extensive research into a range of social care areas and has a particular interest in researching the views of service users. He co-ordinates the MSc in advanced social work with colleagues from Queen's University, Belfast.

Vivian McConvey is a senior professional advisor with First Key (Northern Ireland). Earlier, she worked with Barnardos. Her interests lie in applying the community social work model to children, young people and families. Since qualifying she has been an active exponent of empowerment-based approaches.

Helen Gilmour is a social research worker with the Alzheimer's Society in County Fermanagh. She has been a social worker and care manager with older people. Her research and development interests lie in the field of care for older people living in rural areas.

Tony Viney is a social worker in the community mental health team in the Sperrin Lakeland Health and Social Services Trust where he has developed a specialist interest in issues relating to the social exclusion of people with mental health problems.

Marcella Leonard is an independent social work consultant and trainer. She has a special interest in adult victims of sexual abuse, perpetrators of sexual abuse and their partners, and in psychosexual dysfunctions. She previously worked in the field of mental health, developing specialist expertise in the area of child protection and mental health. Before becoming an independent consultant, she was at the forefront of establishing the programme for the prevention of sexual abuse as senior social worker/ therapist and team co-ordinator.

Marian O'Rourke is a probation officer of sixteen years' experience. Over a number of years she has developed specialist knowledge of working with adult and adolescent sex offenders. She holds the post-qualifying award in social work, an MSc in advanced social work, the advanced award in social work and is currently on secondment from the probation service to the Post Qualifying Education and Training Partnership.

Christine Smyth is a social work education advisor with CCETSW. Earlier she worked in a range of practice, training and development settings in Northern Ireland. She has been actively engaged in developing standards for the personal social services workforce and has published in this area.

George Wilson is an assistant principal social worker for staff development and training in the southern area of Northern Ireland. He has extensive experience of post-qualifying training and is involved in the delivery of a number of programmes including the practice teacher's award and an MSc in advanced social work.

FOREWORD

CCETSW (NI) is pleased to support this publication which gives examples of creative social work practice based on research and theory. Each chapter details a social work project reflecting advanced level practice within CCETSW's post-qualifying framework.

The publication demonstrates the breadth of advanced level practice in the province, with management, training and practice projects all described. The publication highlights the demands of social work at advanced level and the opportunities to tackle complex issues in creative ways. Topical and emotive issues are addressed, and new ways of working are identified which should help other social workers develop their intervention skills.

Advanced level practice is attained by those social workers who can show they have leadership qualities, are innovative and have a sound intellectual knowledge of the social work task. This publication is both a promotion of advanced level practice and a celebration of what has already been achieved in Northern Ireland. I hope it will encourage other social workers to achieve the Advanced Award, thereby improving practice throughout the province.

Mary Stewart
Head of CCETSW Northern Ireland

1 Introduction: social work beyond bureau-professionalism

Stan Houston and Billy McCullough

> So who can be expected to defend the idea of social work? Certainly not employers, nor even Unison or the Association of Directors of Social Services; why should they? It must be active practitioners themselves who take on the task of identifying, refining and celebrating skills.
>
> Meryl Aldridge (1996)

One of the key threats to social work today is a deep descent into a sterile form of 'bureau-professionalism'. Bureau-professionalism can be viewed as a product of the post-Seebohm era of welfare provision in the United Kingdom. It is characterised by a number of defining features. First, it is state-driven. We can see evidence of this in the top-down directives and missives released from central government through a labyrinth of departmental structures. Changes in legislation and policy, which are driven by nascent governments, provoke in their wake a seemingly endless wave of organisational change. We can therefore forgive seasoned practitioners for lapsing into cynicism and a view that nothing is new under the sun when faced with continuing disruption and changing expectations of their daily working role.

Second, bureau-professionalism has come to mean social work by rote. More than at any other time, social work is in the grip of bureaucracy. A challenging problem arises and a new committee is immediately constituted to deal with it. A serious complaint leads to a new procedure which all staff are expected to operationalise with immediate effect. Complex areas of professional practice are reduced to a checklist of elements, units and performance criteria so that new recruits to the service can be appraised through an apparently standardised measure. Put in a different way, we have become a profession of carpenters who, possessing only hammers, have treated every problem as a nail. As a consequence of this bureaucratic mind-set, the time-honoured tradition in social work of investing in 'relationship' has been lost (or at least obscured). Whereas previously we might have approached day-to-day ethical quandaries and fraught situations involving risk and complex need through reasoned and reflective analysis, and an attempt to understand the human condition through relationship building, today we mechanise through the ubiquitous pro forma.

The third feature of bureau-professionalism is its poverty of imagination.

It is as if we are ashamed to compete in the market-place of ideas and engage in legitimate self-promotion as a profession. Aldridge reminds us that:

> social workers need a much greater sense of security – and pride – in their skills which can be built on networks that break out of the quiet desperation of the team, the office and department. Social work was, and is, not one but a portfolio of tasks (p 181).

Unfortunately, mind-sets have been so ingrained within a person-centred paradigm of practice to the detriment of systemic ways of thinking and responding. As a consequence, we have drifted into a 'deficit model' of practice despite the rhetoric of rights and empowerment that pervade so much of our front-stage marketing. Substantive issues, such as social exclusion and the management of complex risk, demand much more than formulaic, reactive responses. Rather, creative problem-solving and innovative remedies require a professional alchemy that is supported and developed by staff-centred, management cultures.

The rupture of the bureau-professional stranglehold in social work is refreshingly displayed throughout the chapters in this book. The contributors, in manifestly different ways, are to be congratulated for taking on the task of identifying, refining and celebrating skills unique to advanced level practitioners: they are the new entrepreneurs of social work. Their work stems from the final year of the MSc in Advanced Social Work – a part-time post-qualifying programme offered jointly by Queen's University Belfast and the University of Ulster. This final year demands of students the production of a dissertation based on a significant piece of research and/or a project examining an area of particular interest within their employing agencies. Concomitant with the demands of advanced level practice, students are required to demonstrate leadership, innovation, independent thinking and intellectual rigour. The presentation of findings from these dissertations – in this short anthology – shows how social work can be at the leading edge of evidence-based interventions. Moreover, it shows imaginative ways of responding to human needs and problems that are far removed from the bureau-professional constraints described earlier.

Thus, in chapter two, McConvey outlines an intergenerational approach to the social support of young single parents. The importance of this work cannot be overstated, for it combines a bottom-up approach to need with an awareness of how informal networks (in this case senior citizens) can play a major role in preventing family breakdown. Similarly, in chapter three, Gilmour explores the relevance of a community development approach to work with older people in a rural environment. Having carried out a small survey of need, the author goes on to describe how she worked in partnership with service users and local agencies to effect change. At the heart of this work is a sensitive understanding of the rights and feelings of older people.

Still within the theme of empowerment, Viney (chapter four) reclaims the forgotten discourse of welfare rights. More specifically, he asserts with firm lucidity the need for a welfare rights strategy in mental health. To the question 'Can social workers in mental health teams... embrace a more radical and strategic approach when combating the material deprivation that faces so many of their clients?', Viney responds affirmatively and unequivocally by demonstrating the fruits of his research and training initiatives with mental health professionals.

Turning from the promotional to the safeguarding domain of practice, two contributors tackle the emotive area of child sexual abuse. In chapter five, Leonard presents her innovative and timely research on perpetrators of child sexual abuse. Tellingly, this research explodes the myth of the isolated and disconnected offender and draws our attention to the reality of continuing contact with family members. Rallying against precipitant, obdurate and alarmist approaches to risk management in this fraught area, Leonard advocates wisely on the necessity of a considered approach to the needs of non-abusing spouses. In chapter six, O'Rourke complements Leonard's position by delineating the process involved in developing a practice manual for work with sex offenders. Reacting against the tendency to approach the supervision of offenders in a procedural, *ad hoc* manner, the manual presents a comprehensive guide that allows the practitioner to build a composite picture of the offender's life. Of challenging import is the author's adherence to a value base which, on the one hand, secures the rights and needs of the victim while, on the other, acknowledges the rights of offenders to lead their lives free from oppression.

The final two chapters in the book point to the organisational context and remind us that advanced level practice follows a range of pathways including management and training. Because of the demanding nature of social work, these chapters underscore the maxim – so easily stated but hard to implement – that staff are the organisation's most precious resource. In chapter seven, Smyth challenges the 'masculinisation' of management by highlighting staff's need for support, supervision and a 'listening ear'. Towards the end of the chapter we are exposed to a model of practice development that dissects the composite elements of staff support and guidance. Finally, in chapter eight, Wilson presents a comprehensive piece of research into the needs of practice teachers within the southern area of Northern Ireland. The recommendations resulting from this research point to the importance of strategic clarity and meaningful forms of support for practice teachers.

We can see from this brief overview that each contributor has identified an unmet need and has exercised leadership, imagination and creativity to address it. Irrespective of the area tackled, what has emerged is a unique process of thinking beyond the confines and taken-for-granted parameters of their daily work. So, instead of the reactive and often apologetic trappings of the bureau-professional, what we see in these examples are professionals who are perspicacious (for example, Leonard's insight into the social circumstances of paedophiles and McConvey's realisation of the potential of intergenerational work). What is more, the attempts to base interventions on research findings (for example, Smyth's and Wilson's qualitative analyses) and to tackle issues of social exclusion (Viney's recognition of the economic marginalisation of mental health users) show that social work can deliver on pressing social imperatives.

To conclude, Lorenz reminds us (1994) that social work is increasingly being affected by globalisation. Put in its starkest terms, globalisation has led to a restructuring of labour markets and a commodification of social relations (where one's rights and privileges are dependent on the market-place). Combined with notable demographic changes across the world (an ageing population and a rupture of traditional family structures), economic globalisation has indelibly contributed to social exclusion in society and the marginalisation of both service users and the social professions. We can therefore look to this anthology for inspiration when faced with these kind of problems in the future.

References

Aldridge, M. (1996) 'Dragged to market: Being a Professional in the Postmodern World', *British Journal of Social Work*, 2, pp 177–94

Lorenz, W. (1994) *Social Work in a Changing Europe*, London: Routledge.

2 An intergenerational approach to the provision of social support to young parents within a community development setting

Vivian McConvey

Introduction

The Poleglass Young Parents' Network was a three-year community-based partnership which ran from January 1996 until December 1999, involving Footprints Women's Centre, the South Eastern Education and Library Board and Barnardos. Throughout the pilot phase of the scheme, young parents participating in the parenting courses began to articulate their need for a strong, local and flexible social support network. They identified needs that ranged from crisis contact to befriending, and assistance with parenting their children. In parallel with this process was a series of requests for assistance from the mothers of the young parents, arising from the pressure and stress of providing financial, practical, social and emotional support for the young parents and their children.

Responding to these demands as co-ordinator of the scheme, I decided to explore in more depth the social support needs of the young parents through a research project. The aim of the research was to investigate the potential of creating a community-based model of social support for young parents within the Poleglass locality.

Poleglass is a relatively recently constructed large urban housing estate on the outskirts of West Belfast. Many of the residents originate from the greater West Belfast area and therefore retain strong connections with their family and friends residing there.

Existing research on the subject identified personal social networks as the most important way in which parents receive most of their practical, emotional and social support in raising their children. The research challenged the social welfare system's reliance on the casework approach. Importantly, Seebohm (1968, pp 476–7) strongly articulated the need to develop a range of models in the provision of support services to families:

> Social work with individuals alone is bound to be of limited effect in an area where the community environment itself is a major impediment to individual development.

Data collected from the Poleglass social support research project concurred with findings of other research in this area. Simply put, the level, accessibility and range of social support within the young parents' locality were identified as key factors in influencing their quality of life. The research project consequently posed three challenges for current social work practice:

1. Social work practice needs to re-evaluate the effectiveness of a casework approach in meeting the complex, diverse individual needs of young parents.
2. Social work practice needs to reassess, value and establish a community's capacity to protect and nurture young parents and their children as a credible model of social support.
3. Social work practice needs to re-evaluate attitudes to older people and acknowledge their huge potential as an untapped natural resource within a community.

Literature review

Extensive research has explored the vital role of social support networks with regard to protecting and nurturing children who are growing up within a stressful environment. The advantages of strengthening personal supports as a means of preventing illness, rather than trying to reduce exposure to the cause of stress, was explored by Cassel (1976). He viewed social support as a buffer, protecting and preventing ill-health brought on as a result of stress factors. Ideally, within a community, the preferred course of action may be to address the factors causing stress and consequently improve quality of health. To bring about change realistically and effectively at this level usually requires a political or socio-economic response. In the absence of such a response, one may be forgiven for thinking that prevention is better than cure.

Research by Garbarino (1979) also suggested that the quality of life in a neighbourhood was a significant indicator of child maltreatment. He suggested that a family in distress might be able to offer their children reasonably good care if they are living within a neighbourhood that provides support through formal and informal networks. Polansky *et al.* (1985) explored this proposition through a study comparing 152 mothers who had been assessed and identified as neglectful and a control group involving 154 non-neglectful mothers. The groups were matched in characteristics including race and social standing. The study findings suggested that neglect was not related to the parents' level of economic impoverishment within their social setting. The major contributing factor reported by neglectful mothers was the 'lack of support' available. Polansky *et al.* (p 274) noted that neglectful mothers 'viewed their locales as less friendly and less helpful; they had fewer people to approach for practical or emotional support'.

The neglectful mothers' group reported a high level of loneliness, social isolation and exclusion, stating they lacked support, for example in simply having someone to talk to in times of crisis. They viewed their neighbourhood as less friendly and less helpful, which meant they had few people to turn to in a time of crisis for practical or emotional support, and 'they lived lonelier lives'.

In exploring the factors which might influence the quality of child care within disadvantaged poor neighbourhoods, Polansky *et al.* concluded that two major factors impacted on parents' ability to meet their children's needs: first, they feel emotionally supported, and second, they are not lonely. The findings of this study proposed a change in social work practice. This involved re-evaluating the preferred individual casework model by exploring how social work practice could be more effective if a community approach was embraced. Through such an approach, Polansky *et al.* (p 274) suggested:

> Workers can then identify formal and informal support systems that might help. The role becomes one of liaison, helper, advocate, resource mobiliser, and consultant to overcome barriers to the participation of the families that concern us.

Coohey (1996), in reviewing research relating to social support and the maltreatment of children, identified three factors as possible indicators of maltreatment: the size of the network, the number of contacts a person had, and proximity to neighbours. Coohey concurred with the findings of Polansky *et al.* that neglectful mothers had fewer contacts overall, and had much less contact with members within their support network. Given this understanding of the impact of the quality of the social environment on the mother's mental health and well-being, research has demonstrated the importance of creating a strong, resourceful and flexible support network. Whilst a support network will provide a buffer to the environmental stresses faced by parents, the quality of support provided by that network can significantly influence social and health outcomes. Coohey (p 245) further proposes that 'an investigation of the parents' network properties could then be used to understand why parents receive fewer resources'.

Context of practice

The Young Parents' Network initiative developed out of Barnardos' practice experience with young mothers at the PACT (Parent and Child Together) project. The PACT project had ten years' experience of working with vulnerable teenage parents in a residential and community setting. The majority of the young mothers were perceived as vulnerable: their own histories may have included care, abuse in childhood, difficulties in establishing relationships, and involvement in 'dangerous' or self-abusive behaviours. Experience at PACT showed that the transition into the community was difficult and could be overwhelming, even with the provision of a high level of after-care support. The after-care service had noted that young parents continually expressed feelings of isolation and vulnerability and did not use the community support available or have family networks to draw upon.

In response, Barnardos undertook an audit of community-based supports for young parents in Northern Ireland. During the audit process, several agencies expressed an interest in working in partnership to assess the needs of this group and possibly develop joint initiatives. The Poleglass Young Parents' Network was one of the initiatives in which Barnardos negotiated a three-pilot partnership project involving the statutory, voluntary and community sectors. The aim was to provide a range of locality-based community support models to young parents. The Young Parents' Network represented a movement into community development – a new area of work for Barnardos. The project would test a model of work, adopting a bottom-up as opposed to a top-down approach. This approach was deemed to be more responsive in identifying and addressing local unmet needs and developing new ways of providing services that other agencies working independently had found problematic: it was believed that no one agency working in isolation could meet the diverse, complex and individual needs of young parents. The Young Parents' Network model combined direct practice with an impact strategy. In the practice element the development worker, assisted by a co-worker, facilitated a four-phase programme, comprising:

- a twenty-week groupwork programme including personal development and parenting skills
- the development of a peer support model to identify the support needs of the young parents within the locality, for example a drop-in centre
- accessing pre-vocational training, in which young parents could redress lost educational and employment opportunities
- promoting empowerment by providing the skills and knowledge required by the young parents to ensure they were proactively involved in the management of the project.

The impact strategy involved influencing policy and practice in this area. In doing so, it also attempted to address the wider political, social and economic factors linked to the provision of services.

Research aims and objectives

The aim of the research was to investigate, within the Poleglass Young Parents' Network, the potential of creating a community-based model of social support for young parents and their children by providing a volunteer scheme involving older people as friendly grandparents. This aim was translated into three objectives:

- to identify community social supports required by young parents and their children
- to test out if the social support needs of young parents could be met through the provision of a grandparent volunteer scheme within the Young Parents' Network
- to assess the potential of the members of the Poleglass Senior Citizens' Club to become involved in a grandparent volunteering scheme.

Methodology

The research project elicited the views of two sample groups: young parents attending the project and older people involved in the Footprints Senior Citizens' Club who would potentially provide the friendly grandparent volunteers. In relation to the former group, the Poleglass Young Parents' Network project had contact with eighteen young parents who had completed the twenty-week formal parenting course and were currently attending the drop-in centre or the toy and book library.

A letter explaining the research and requesting their participation was sent to every young parent, with a reply slip and a stamped addressed envelope. Nine young parents out of the potential research population of eighteen agreed to participate. Each completed an individual questionnaire and participated in a semi-structured interview that explored elements of the questionnaire in more depth. A video presentation exploring the potential of older people as volunteers was also shown to the group.

Adhering to a community development model in the creation of new services, the research project explored the potential of finding volunteer grandparents within the Footprints Women's Centre. The Centre had a strong, well-established Senior Citizens' Club, which worked closely with the young parents, jointly hosting presentations for funders, politicians and external agencies. The Senior Citizens' Club met on Thursday evenings in the Women's Centre. Membership numbers were 18 to 20, aged from 60 to 83. The senior citizens agreed to participate in a semi-structured focus group discussion. The large group was broken into three smaller groups and three researchers facilitated the discussion.

The research project was mainly qualitative because this methodology is most suited to tackling questions such as how people feel about issues, what they think and how they make decisions in their everyday lives. The issues addressed were essentially practice-orientated, exploring problem-solving in a social context, and therefore did not generate data that could be easily analysed. The central research question was 'Do young parents require a strong, flexible, local social support network and if so, can older people from the locality acting as volunteer grandparents provide such a service?'

Results

The data were collected through questionnaires completed during the individual interviews with the young parents (9) and a semi-structured focus group with the older people (20).

Figure 2.1 Age of parents

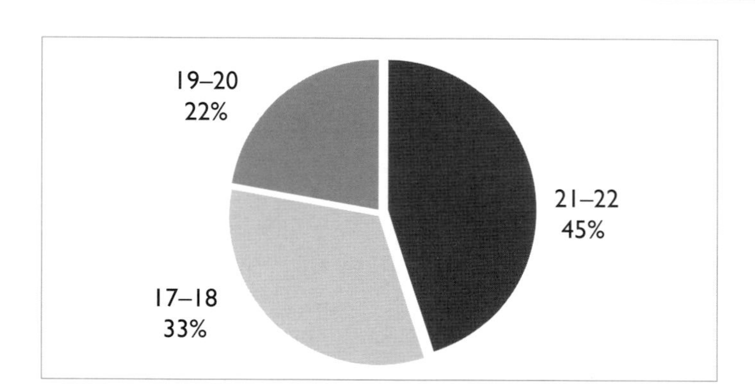

Figure 2.2 Age of children

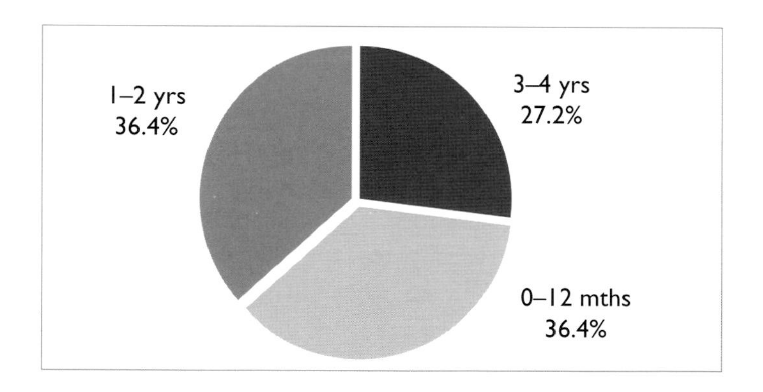

The youngest of the nine parents who participated were aged 17, although the project involved 15 and 16 year-olds, but they declined to take part. Of the research sample of eleven children 73 per cent were aged under 2. The youngest was five days old.

Figure 2.3 Causes of stress (number of people responding)

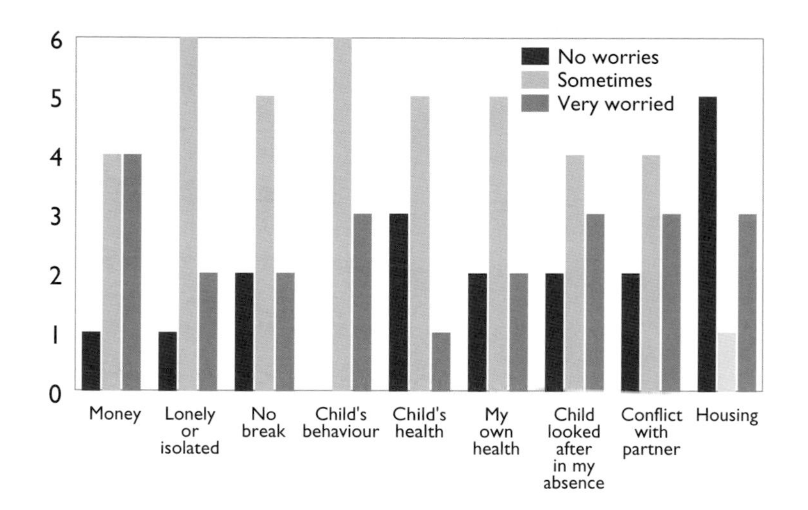

Respondents were requested to rate their levels of stress in relation to specific areas. The results of these questions are shown in Figure 2.3. 'Feeling lonely and isolated' was rated highly with 89 per cent of respondents identifying this as a significant source of stress. 'Lack of a supportive network' and feeling isolated may have contributed to the fact that 78 per cent of respondents felt it was difficult to get a break from the children. Respondents noted that levels of stress within the home had a negative impact on children's behaviour.

Figure 2.4 Social support networks

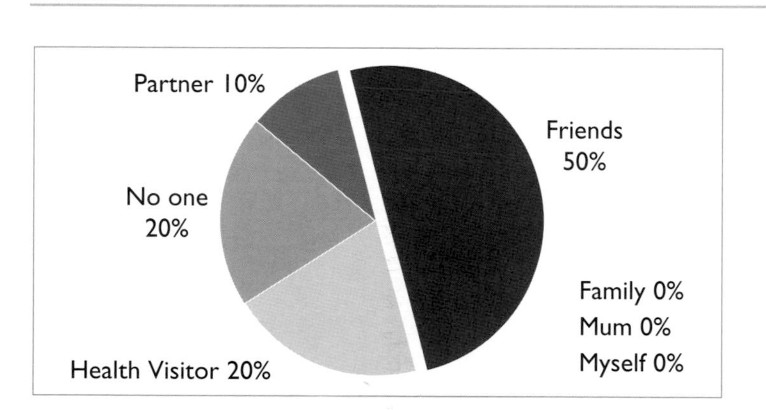

Asked if they had someone to listen to them, 50 per cent of the young parents said that friends filled this role. Alarmingly, 20 per cent of respondents indicated that they did not have anyone who listened to them at all.

Figure 2.5 Unmet needs

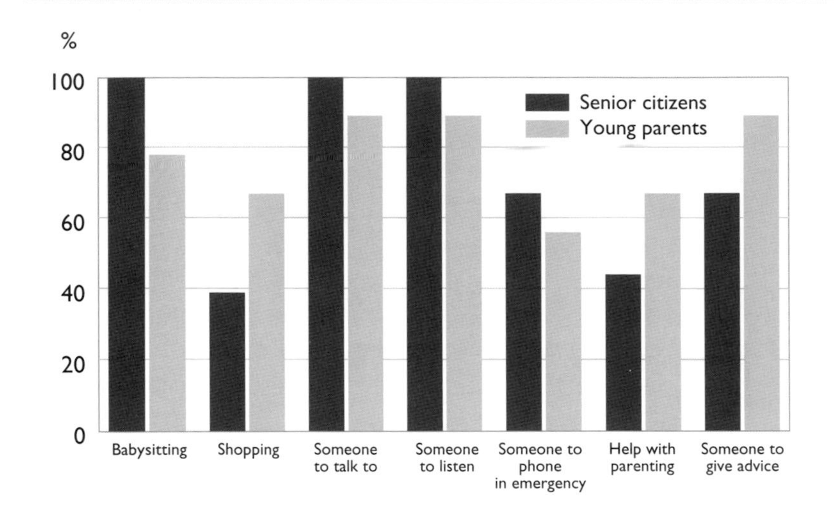

Figure 2.6 Comparing unmet needs with potential resources

Type of support required	**Young parents' support needs**	**Senior citizens' assessment of support available**
Help with children	• getting a break • access to crèche facilities • short notice child-minding • babysitting	• look after children and give advice about child-rearing • take children for walks • babysitting • advice with problems with children
Emotional support	• someone to talk to • someone who listens • someone to socialise with • someone to confide in	• someone to talk to • someone with time to listen
Practical help	• to decorate house • to fix broken things • to do housework when sick • help with short-term loans	• someone to help with money problems

The research compared the needs of young parents with the type of supports that could be provided through a friendly grandparent volunteer scheme. Figures 2.5 and 2.6 demonstrate a clear correlation between the support needs of young parents and the potential social support resources that volunteer grandparents could provide. Both groups indicated that a key role might be that of confidant and listener. This finding was significant given that one fifth of participants had indicated that they did not have access to anyone who would listen to them.

Figure 2.7 Young parents' reaction to volunteer grandparents (number of people responding in each category)

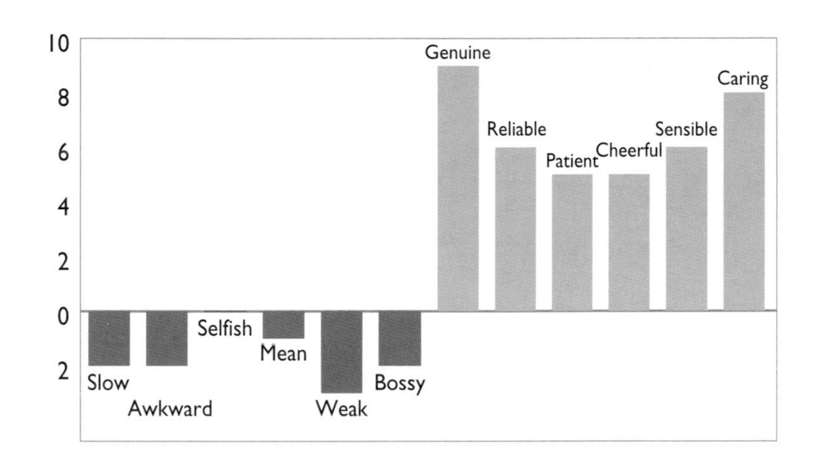

The young parents' view of older people was extremely positive, as shown in Figure 2.7. They rated older people highly, viewing them as genuine, caring, reliable and sensible. Negative qualities related to the young parents' assessment of the impact of health on their well-being. Terms such as 'weak', 'slow' and 'awkward' were viewed as being related to physical ability. The findings indicated that the young parents were very open to accessing assistance from volunteer grandparents.

Implications for practice

The Poleglass research respondents were requested to rate the level of stress in nine areas of their life: money, feeling isolated or lonely, not getting a break from the children, the child's behaviour, the child's health, their own health, child-minding, housing and conflict with partner. Their responses indicated that they were subjected to high levels of stress arising from their social situation. They stated that stress greatly impacted upon their health and well-being, but more particularly on the quality of care they were able to provide for their children. Gingerbread (1996, p 56) conducted a survey across Northern Ireland, and the findings indicated that:

> ...nearly all the lone parents who participated in this research were affected by the nature of their situation. Although a young population, they suffer high levels of fatigue and debilitating effects on physical and emotional well-being.

The Poleglass research results concur with the Gingerbread findings and those reviewed in the literature by Cassel (1976), Garbarino (1979) and Polansky et al. (1985). Each argues that families in distress require a range of additional support models in order to provide 'reasonable good care' for their children. These findings have major implications for current social work practice, in particular the need for statutory agencies to aspire to provide early preventive help and assistance that aims to empower young parents to develop and maintain a strong flexible support network. To achieve this aspiration, statutory services need to consider and address the following three challenges in relation to social work practice:

- to re-evaluate the effectiveness of a casework approach in meeting the complex, diverse individual needs of young parents
- to reassess, value and establish a community's capacity to protect and nurture young parents and their children as a credible model of social support
- to re-evaluate their attitudes towards older people and acknowledge this group's huge potential as an untapped natural resource in a community.

The first challenge demands that social work should question why community social work has not been developed or supported to the same degree as casework within family and childcare provision. Historically, there has been a consistent push to embrace a community approach, though any substantial practice development in this area has not materialised. This is contrary to the support for such a model provided by three major social reviews, the Seebohm Report (1968), the Barclay Report (1980), and the Griffiths Report (1988). Since the late 1960s there has been a continuing debate within social work circles between client-centred and community-based approaches. Seebohm (para 2) consolidated support for community social work, suggesting that:

> it will enable the greatest possible number of individuals to act reciprocally, giving and receiving services for the well-being of the whole community.

It is more than thirty years since Seebohm suggested the need for departments to gain an understanding and knowledge of their local community and voluntary resources. He was proposing that social workers should develop skills in formal and informal networking, encouraging participation through the provision of local forums of community representatives, service users and volunteers. The Barclay Committee (1980), set up by the National Institute for Social Work, reiterated Seebohm's vision by calling for a wider brief for social services. The report proposed broadening the traditional approach to encompass 'social care planning' and more indirect service provision. Barclay proposed that social work practice should, in working with individuals and groups, directly link into local networks, supporting and enhancing their development.

Findings from this research demonstrated that respondents were subjected to high levels of stress arising from issues such as feeling isolated or lonely, children's behaviour and not getting a break. Finding solutions to such complex issues demands more than an individual casework approach. Building confidence, skills, knowledge and connecting the young parent directly into community supports provides an opportunity to address issues on many levels. The young parents who were first introduced to the Poleglass Women's Centre through the Young Parents' Network quickly learnt how to access much more than a two-hour parenting programme. They joined the education classes, got involved in the drop-in centre, used the crèche and joined the after-schools project. More importantly, when shopping in the local supermarket or walking through the estate, they were greeted by new friendly faces.

So, the question may be 'Can we embrace a new model of social work, or have we advanced so far with one model of work that it would be impossible to change policy, practice, legislation and attitudes?' If a new model can be embraced then implementing change requires the development of new practice models, with the emphasis on inter-agency working, developing new initiatives, establishing networks of support, but most importantly working proactively to ensure services are close to the community.

The second challenge, to re-evaluate a community's capacity to protect and nurture young parents and their children, builds on the previous arguments for a community social work approach. The Poleglass research findings identified stress as a result of isolation and loneliness as a major factor impacting on the quality of life. This analysis concurred with and supported learning from the researcher's practice experience in the Young Parents' Network Project. In the parenting courses particular sessions were dedicated to exploring parenthood, support networks and relationships. During the sessions young parents described feelings of loneliness and isolation as a result of their new parenting role. New responsibilities tended to accelerate their transition into the adult world. Relationships with peers suffered greatly as a result. Alarmingly, 20 per cent of research participants did not have anyone who acted as a confidant and good listener (Figure 2.4), while for 50 per cent of respondents friends filled this role. The role of friends was quite significant, as young parents acknowledged the vital services they provided outside the family network. This was interesting given the fact that young parents who attended the Young Parents' Network Project parenting courses related loneliness and isolation to lack of peer friendship. Attendance at the project had significantly increased their social network by creating close friendships with other young parents, young people and women. The Young Parents'

Network Project supported members to connect with their community.

Key to this process was the partnership nature of the project. The project provided a range of services by utilising the community infrastructure within the locality. It offered access to a listening ear, new friends, information, advice, guidance, a crèche, educational opportunities and links into other community groups. The Women's Centre and the Young Parents' Network were viewed by the research respondents as important sources of emotional support and guidance. The services provided met their needs in relation to personal development and confidence-building. Both organisations explored the core of the young parents' problems and offered a range of solutions and opportunities to bring about change. They supervised and nurtured the growth and development of mother and child. In doing so, many problems, issues and challenges were absorbed by the project and the centre. Consequently, this negated the need to contact social services. As Bowan (1997, p 11) clearly articulates:

> Any parent, anywhere, can hit a patch when the job seems more than they can cope with... When you are feeling low, the regular, dependable visit of your special home visitor can be a big help. What is often needed at this stage is not a professional worker at all but a good friend who can listen sympathetically, give practical help and encouragement and enable the family to come out, to make use of the facilities in their community and to meet other parents.

The final challenge that needs to be addressed is to re-evaluate attitudes towards older people and acknowledge their huge potential as an untapped natural resource within a community. One factor influencing the value we place on older people in society is the continual reference to the increasing burden the older population is going to place on younger ones in the future. Therefore, in the main, the contribution to society by older people is not realised. The Poleglass research results challenge social work to re-evaluate older people and to view them not only as consumers but as a valuable community resource. The research confirmed the original hypothesis that older people are an 'untapped natural resource'. Family members of different ages have learnt from one another since time and families began. Today, due to divorce, increasing mobility, and the growth of lone-parent families, young people often lack the extended family that helped during difficult times. A significant number of young children have never had the opportunity to form a close relationship with an older person. Grandparenting activity is not only for biological grandparents, it is a vital function that links older people to life and social usefulness.

The concept of social support was new for the senior citizens who participated in the research. They believed traditional forms of social support had been eroded, necessitating more formal types of support. When they were parents, social support was a natural and ongoing process, integrated into their daily lives. Everyone was 'in the same boat' and therefore neighbours 'looked after each other'. Their experience was one of the whole community striving to survive, clothe and feed the children. Quietly and unobtrusively the neighbours shared everything, including food.

The research findings outlined above compared the responses given by the senior citizens and the young parents in relation to broad support areas (see Figures 2.5 and 2.6). The two groups were in agreement in the areas of babysitting and having someone to listen to and confide in. Volunteer grandparents viewed themselves as having a key role in alleviating the isolation and loneliness of young parents through providing emotional support. In fact the relationship would be reciprocal, given that the literature points to high levels of loneliness and isolation among older people.

Young parents scored older people highly in terms of their personal qualities (see Figure 2.7). Their picture and experience of grandparents was positive, with many fond memories of their own grandparents. This attitude was evidenced in answers relating to the support and help grandparents could offer. Apart from practical childcare help, the young parents rated quite highly the experience and knowledge grandparents had to offer. They believed grandparents could 'give advice about rearing children', 'show me what children need' and 'give advice with problems with children'.

The research resulted in a recommendation to set up a grandparent volunteer scheme and applying to the Age Concern Millennium Awards and Children in Need, to fund the project. An example of such provision is the US Foster Grandparents Programme, part of the Corporation for National Service. It began in 1965 and originally was planned to alleviate poverty amongst older Americans. The programme currently involves 25,000 older volunteers on low incomes, who work with 100,000 vulnerable children and young people every day. Each volunteer receives a tax-exempt expense of £2.45 an hour, and is contracted to work twenty hours a week, usually five half-days. Volunteers work in schools, assisting with literacy skills, counselling young people involved in the justice system and assisting children with disabilities. Participants are 60 years old and over, with 34 per cent between 60 and 69, 50 per cent between 70 and 79 and 16 per cent over 80. Irving (1998) noted about the US Foster Grandparents Programme that:

> Foster grandparents have an excellent record of long-term service and time-keeping – they are only too aware that these children, above all, need their

> commitment... Forming intense, personal bonds with the individual children was easy and natural for most of the older people. Foster grandparents' parenting has a very positive impact on the child's development in both intellectual and social areas.

Such schemes challenge our attitudes and expectations of older people. The Poleglass research demonstrated a need for friendly grandparents and the senior citizens believed they could adequately meet that need.

In conclusion, it is evident that the range and level of support required by young parents cannot be provided effectively by any one agency working in isolation. The challenges, dilemmas, problems and issues related to supporting young parents are complex and the solutions require social work intervention not only on an individual level but also on a community level. The changes advocated for in social work practice are not unachievable. Jack (1997), in reviewing the Canklow Estate Project in Rotherham, argues that change is possible and does produce unexpected outcomes. The Rotherham local authority funding the project had a team of community social workers based in the community centre. Their caseload was made up of children in care, on supervision orders and on the child protection register. The social work model of intervention involved (p 117):

> the development and maintenance of various formal and informal support networks. The team initiated women's groups, play schemes, adult education classes and youth clubs.

Through evaluation the project demonstrated 'marked reductions in the number of children "in care" and on supervision orders and, most significantly, a drop to almost zero of children on the child protection register'.

Canklow Estate Project demonstrated how social support networks could enhance the quality of life for a family and reduce the stresses on parents and their children. Social workers providing locally based services, such as child care, parenting courses, advice, support, and education and training, did impact significantly on a family and community. Social work practitioners and agencies in Northern Ireland must now question how ready they are to test out such approaches.

References

Barclay Report (1992) 'Social Workers: Their Role and Tasks', Report of a Working Party, London: Bedford Square

Bowan, F. (1997) 'Help at home for parents under stress. Scottish Home Visiting Development Project', *The Scottish Child*, 1(2)

Cassel, J. (1976) 'The contribution of the social; environment to host resistance', *American Journal of Epidemiology*, 102, 107–23

Coohey, C. (1996) 'Child maltreatment: testing the social isolation hypothesis', *Child Abuse and Neglect*, Vol. 20 No 3, pp 241–54

Garbarino, J. and Crouter, A. (1979) 'Defining community context for Parent Child relationships: The correlates of child maltreatment', *Child Development* 49:604–16

Gingerbread (1997) 'A Wise Head On Young Shoulders, the experience of young lone parents', Belfast: Gingerbread

Irving, E. (1998) 'Life Experience as a Resource', conference paper presented at Investing in the Future – Promoting and Safeguarding Children's Early Experience, March 1998

Irving, E. (1998) Services Resource Pack, Trans Age Action, Age Concern England

Jack, G. (1997) 'An ecological approach to social work with children and families', *Children and Family Social Work*, 2, pp 109–20

Polansky, N., Gaudin, J., Ammons, P., and Davis, K. (1985) 'The Psychological Ecology of the Neglectful Mother', *Child Abuse and Neglect*, Vol. 9, pp 265–75

Seebohm, F. (1968) Report of the Committee on Local Authority and Allied Personal Social Services, London: HMSO

3 Older people and community development: is there a role for social work?

Helen Gilmour

Introduction

Two of the major focal areas of discussion within Health and Social Services are introduced in this chapter. The first is the growing debate about the needs of older people arising from demographic, political and economic pressures (Hughes, 1995; Tester, 1996). The second is the significant re-emergence of a community development approach:

> Community development has a particularly important contribution to make in reaching and involving people in need, in encouraging active participation by local communities in needs assessment and in seeking to maximise the participation of service users. (DHSS, 1996:2.6)

Combining these two imperatives it is therefore pertinent to ask the question: Is a community development approach relevant to social work with older people?

Responding affirmatively to this question, this chapter explores the relevance of community development and its application to work with older people through the description and analysis of one project instigated and managed by the author. The project centred on work carried out in a small rural village (Derrylin) in which a twelve-unit sheltered housing complex for older people – Clachan Court – had just opened. It follows through the links made with the local community development association, Oaklee Housing Association, who built the complex, Helpline/Aidcall and social services. More specifically, it describes the small but innovative developments that were undertaken to support older people living in this rural area.

A short review of relevant policy and literature in relation to social work with older people and community development sets this practice in context. This section is followed by a description and analysis of the project, how it was set up and managed; it is here that the author outlines some of the social work processes that were enacted with the key stakeholders. The chapter concludes by analysing, in a more general sense, the implications of these findings for social work practice.

Literature review

The publication *People First* (DHSS (NI), 1990) focused on the concept of care in the community. It included an assessment procedure, which emphasised a person remaining in the community supported by a package of care. However, Hughes believes that this approach has isolated the older person from his or her social context; thus, the care plan meets individual need but does not address the wider inequalities of class, gender or race. Evans and Kearing (1996) echo this warning against adopting an individualistic approach to social work. They believe that the roots of such an approach lie in the pressurised work environment in which the social work practitioner operates. Instead, Hughes recommends that practitioners and managers should adopt a professional model of community care, which is based on a holistic approach, recognising the interconnected nature of the needs of older people.

Similarly, Bland (1996) promotes an empowering and anti-ageist approach to work with older people pointing out that the potential of older people to influence policies and services has not yet been realised. She feels that the social worker holds the key to working creatively in partnership with older people and their carers and concludes that 'there is no field of social work in which empowerment is more urgent and requires more skill than with very old people' (p 213).

Clarke (1996), in his analysis of community care policies, social work and community development, suggests that the links between social work and community-based approaches have never been adequately debated. Historically, the Barclay Report (1983) supported a community-orientated approach by emphasising the need for social workers to identify informal networks of care in the community. Echoing many of its themes, Clarke sets out a preventive, community development approach within social work, including a model for 'the conceptualisation, planning and analysis of action'.

Moreover, Smale (1998) cogently describes social services as either aid- or development-focused. Put another way, he believes agencies fulfil the role of carrying water to drought-stricken areas or of working alongside people to dig irrigation schemes. Preferring the latter approach, Smale suggests that we make use of the wealth of information that has already been gathered about communities and consult with service users to ensure the development of more effective practice.

Importantly, the social work role within community development must be able to integrate what Payne (1996) describes as the three main strands of social work: the personal, professional and political. Lorenz (1994) believes an integration of this kind will result in different types of approach and action without diminishing social work's professional and ethical standing. He states:

> Social work competence will increasingly depend on practitioners being able to account for their answers to these questions – with reference to their own understanding as to where the profession has its place in society and how this came about, what the limitations are and where its opportunities for changing and transforming these limitations lie (p 172).

Context of practice

The setting of this project is in County Fermanagh, which is described as 'a place of beauty and tranquillity with a rich historical past' (Fermanagh Economic Development Strategy, pp 95–9). It is a dispersed rural community with a population of 54,033 (Northern Ireland Census, 1991). Fourteen per cent of the population are aged 65 and over and almost 30 per cent of this group live alone.

The Sperrin Lakeland Health and Social Services Trust became operational in 1996. The social work elderly care team within the Trust is based in the county town of Enniskillen and is responsible for specific geographic patches. In line with the introduction of care management in April 1993, social workers also act as care managers and are responsible for co-ordinating multi-disciplinary assessments and creating, costing and reviewing care plans. Grass-roots practitioners are encouraged by their managers to maintain and develop links with local community groups; however, there is no one with the sole responsibility for community development.

The project began at the time of the opening of Clachan Court. Oaklee Housing is a registered charity and a lead provider of sheltered housing. Derrylin village is eleven miles from Enniskillen and close to the border with the Republic. The 1991 census figures indicate that there were 365 older people in the village, 100 of them living alone. This area ranks poorly on socio-economic indices and is positioned within the worst 16 per cent in the deprivation ranking of wards in Northern Ireland (Robson Intensity Scores). The village population is primarily Catholic (approximately 77 per cent) and has suffered due to civil unrest and sectarianism. There are close neighbourhood relationships but, tellingly, no community-owned social facilities in the village.

Aim of the project

The aim of the project was to undertake research and development at Clachan Court to improve the lives of older people in the area. To initiate the project, a small survey of the needs of these older people was undertaken. Building on the survey's findings, the main objectives of the project were then to:

- instigate a partnership approach involving older people, the housing association, the local community development association and social

services to address expressed needs through appropriate service development. A pre-condition of this work was that it was to be underpinned by anti-discriminatory (and in particular, anti-ageist) values
- describe fully, accurately and realistically the milestones reached and the challenges faced as the project evolved and, through reflection on the processes involved, make recommendations regarding the social work role within community development.

Methodology

Reflecting the aims and objectives above, the methodology and outcomes of the project were broken into two phases. Because a basic premise in community and service development is the necessity of involving people in defining their own needs, phase one of the project commenced with a needs analysis. The second phase attempted to address the findings by working in partnership with identified stakeholders to bring about change.

More specifically, in phase one the author designed a short questionnaire divided into sections covering personal details, services provided, and health and care needs, for example 'In an emergency situation who do you generally call on with your lifeline/helpline?' Following discussion involving social services, the community development association, Oaklee Housing and Helpline/Aidcall alarm personnel, it was agreed to disseminate the questionnaire to the 21 people living within a three-mile radius of Clachan Court who used a Helpline/Aidcall alarm system. Eleven of these people were already known to social services and either the social work assistant or the author completed the questionnaire during a home visit. Of the group not known to social services only one person agreed to take part in the survey when approached by the alarm systems personnel by telephone. This contrasting level of participation underlined the importance of a user-sensitive approach in the research.

Results

As presented in Figure 3.1, eleven women and one man took part in the survey. This in part reflects the balance of the sexes in the wider population in which there are more women than men. Women are also twice as likely as men to live alone (Tinker, 1992).

Figure 3.1 Breakdown of respondents by gender

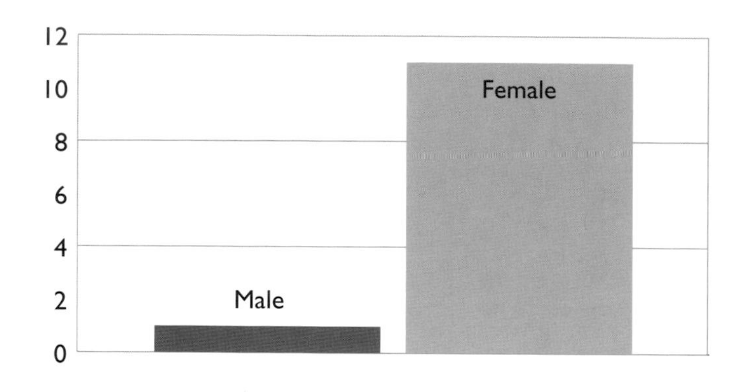

Figure 3.2 indicates that almost all (11 out of 12) of the people surveyed were in receipt of full attendance allowance and were therefore deemed to need frequent attention or continual supervision by day and night. These results compare with the 29.3 per cent of the elderly population in Northern Ireland who are in receipt of attendance allowance at either the full or daily rate (Age Concern, 1995) and indicates the targeting of the service to a highly dependent group.

Figure 3.2 Breakdown of respondents in receipt of attendance allowance

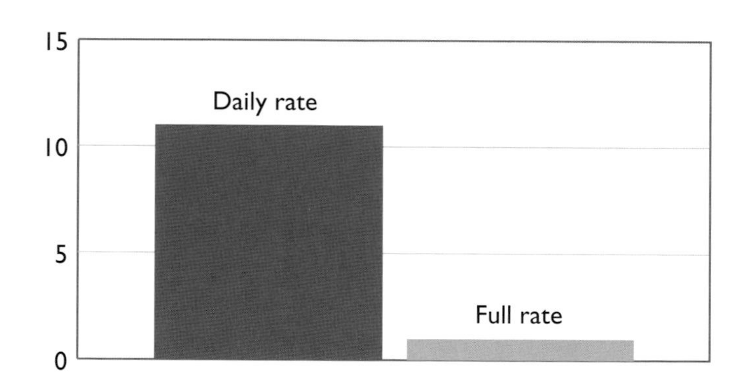

All the people surveyed were in receipt of income support, indicating a high level of material deprivation. This compares strikingly with the Northern Ireland average of 25 per cent and the UK average of 16.1 per cent of people in receipt of income support. All indicated some type of health problem: seven out of the twelve stated they suffered from arthritis; other conditions were pernicious anaemia, hypertension, bronchial asthma, multiple sclerosis, previous strokes, gall-stones and sensory disabilities. These results were higher than the local profile which shows 38 per cent of elderly people in the Fermanagh District Council area suffering from a long-term illness (WHSSB/ NIHE Workshop, 1997).

Half the people stated that in the event of an emergency they would contact a member of the family, using their present alarm system, as illustrated in Figure 3.3. Three said they would contact family and neighbours and a further three would contact neighbours solely.

Figure 3.3 Emergency contact person

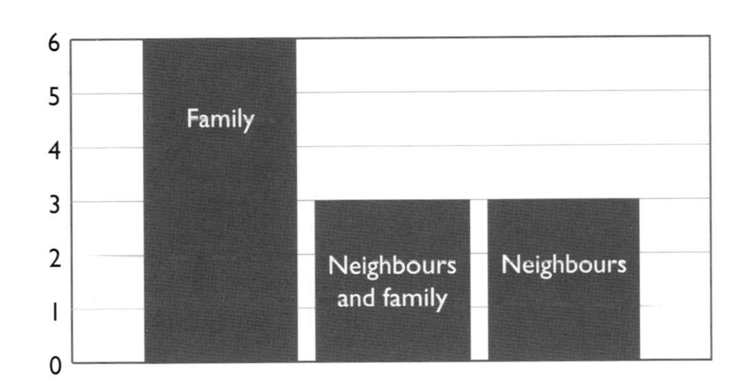

These results reflect recent research (Gilmour, 1997) which indicated a high level of family and neighbourly contact in this rural area. This particular piece of research cannot comment, however, on the quality of such relationships.

Finally, none of the people surveyed suggested that there were any needs that the new warden of Clachan Court could help them meet. The results may also reflect other research indicating that older people do not like to complain about services or the lack of them (Walker and Warren, 1996). This research cannot confirm that they had no unmet needs, but the majority of people did ask who the warden was: the post had not been filled at the time of the survey.

Two-thirds of the people interviewed, however, were interested in the development of social functions in Clachan Court. This interest in attending social functions became a clear focus for development work and constituted phase two of the project. To take forward this aspiration, the community development association was approached for possible names of volunteers within the local area who would be interested in working with the residents. It was made clear at the outset that the intention was to achieve a cross-community group. Six out of the seven potential volunteers said they would be interested in becoming involved. The newly-established volunteer bureau in Fermanagh was also approached. This contact had a positive outcome resulting in the co-ordinator agreeing to provide some informal training on setting up a voluntary group and the nature of voluntary work.

The initial meeting of this small group provided clues about expectations and backgrounds. Even where people sat in the room reflected the religious divide. It was also difficult to manage a meeting in which some people were unused to the protocol of not speaking simultaneously. As such, the author needed to draw on social work skills including negotiation and conflict management to manage the process effectively. Subsequent meetings gradually became more relaxed and conducive. Nevertheless, the work in this phase required sensitive handling, and the ability to develop relationships creatively and act as a catalyst and encourager.

The result of this second phase was the establishment of a committee with a written constitution, made up of local people, of whom half were aged over 60. Although none of the Protestants were willing to hold an elected position, the group was cross-community. A weekly coffee-morning was set up, with up to thirty older people from the local area attending. Two older people who lived only a couple of miles apart met for the first time after forty years. By the end of project the committee was well established and funding was being sought for a craft afternoon. Two of the committee members became regular visitors of some of the new residents in Clachan Court.

Implications for practice

The Clachan Court project, though small in scale, was significant for social work practice in three ways. First, community development grows from alliances that are formed between appropriate bodies and people. Such an approach is recognised and encouraged by the current government as a way of promoting health and social well-being. Social workers with their interpersonal and networking skills should take a lead role in community development, working alongside statutory, community and voluntary groups. This approach contrasts with the individual casework method that is often based on a medical model of the needs of older people, resulting in their isolation from their neighbours. Social workers can instigate the building of wider community relationships with the inclusion of vulnerable people in service development plans, as evidenced in this project. As a result, services can be developed for people living in disadvantaged areas. This project demonstrates that anti-ageist and anti-sectarian values can be promoted within the context of building partnerships. The context may be limited and compromise may be necessary, but the outcome can bring about positive change.

Second, in developing services for people, it is vital that they are consulted and their views sought. Consultation, research and needs analysis necessitates specified time and skills, particularly in the field of working with older people. A personal approach which provides quality time is vital. In this project this was patently illustrated by the people surveyed, with a very poor level of response to a 'stranger' on a telephone in comparison to the full acceptance of a home visit during which important information was gained. Developing practice, which genuinely promotes user involvement, cannot be carried out unless time is invested in forming and sustaining relationships with service users. Frequently, aspirations of empowering service users in decision-making processes are not matched with reality because such processes are time-consuming, resource-intensive and require creative action. In this project empowerment was achieved through the development of a small local community group, of whom half the members were retired. Perhaps this example can provide a model for other spheres of work with the use of advocates found in the local community.

Third, adopting a community development approach revealed a wealth of hidden resources that were already to be found in the community and particularly in the so-called 'active retired' group. The findings of the project indicate that community and voluntary groups can work in partnerships with social services to help meet the social care needs of older people. However, this should not be a substitute for properly resourced government provision for those with a high level of care needs. But within a mixed economy of care we should be alert to the tensions and ambiguities that do exist in relation to responsibilities and where they lie. The Clachan Court project shows how these responsibilities can be balanced by demonstrating that social work practitioners can use community development to bring about positive change. This method of intervention must recognise the contributions people within a community can make, regardless of their age. These range from vocalising needs to practical voluntary work.

This project commends the role that social workers (with their specialised skills and knowledge) can play in helping local communities recognise and use their potential to help themselves, thus championing genuine care in and by the community. This requires social workers to acknowledge and promote their wealth of expertise, and the humility to accept and encourage a wider community involvement. Social workers saturated in the values of empowerment, skilled in the building and sustaining of relationships and in touch with the most vulnerable in society, should be at the cutting edge of community development.

References

Age Concern, NI (1995) 'The Needs Of Older People', Briefing Paper, Age Concern: Belfast

Barclay Report (1982) 'Social Workers: Their Roles and Tasks', London: Bedford Square Press

Bland, R. (1996) 'Developing Services For Older People and Their Families'. *Research Highlights in Social Work*, No. 29, London: Jessica Kingsley Publishers

Clarke, S. (1996) *Social Work as Community Development*, London: Avebury

DHSS (1990) *People First – Community Care in Northern Ireland*, Belfast: HMSO

DHSS (1996) *Health and WellBeing: Into The Next Millennium (Regional Strategy for Health And Social Wellbeing 1997–2002)*, Belfast: HMSO

Evans, D. and Kearing I. (1996) *Working in Social Care A Systematic Approach*, Aldershot: Arena

Fermanagh Economic Development Strategy (1995–1999), P. Quinn Consultancy Services

Gilmour, H. (1997) 'Day Centre Care Portrait and Potential', Unpublished

Hughes, B. (1995) *Older People And Community Care*, Buckingham: Open University

Lorenz, W. (1994) *Social Work in a Changing Europe*, London: Routledge

Northern Ireland Housing Executive and Northern Ireland Federation Housing Association (1997) 'Housing With Care', Scoping Paper, Belfast

Payne, M. (1995) *Social Work in Community Care*, London: Macmillan

Smale, G. (1998) 'Developing Role In Community Care', No. 1211 (Social Exclusion Supplement) 26 Feb–4 March

Tester, S. (1996) *Community Care for Older People*, London: Macmillan

Tinker, A. (1992) *Elderly People In Modern Society*, London: Longman

Walker, I. and Warren, L. (1996) *Changing Services for Older People*, Buckingham: Open University

4 Slipping through the safety net? Towards a welfare rights strategy in mental health

Tony Viney

Introduction

The aim of this chapter is to identify the need for a welfare rights strategy in mental health. Initially, the author briefly considers current research and debates concerning poverty and its links with mental ill-health. The paucity of research in the area of welfare rights within multi-disciplinary mental health teams is also highlighted. Then, through a discussion of a research and training initiative undertaken in Sperrin Lakeland Health and Social Services Trust, the author demonstrates the need for a more coherent welfare rights strategy in mental health. He also argues for a more innovative and radical role for social workers responding to the issue of poverty.

Gaps in research

Research into the area of poverty and mental health has both strengths and limitations. On the one hand, the debate over the nature of poverty has shifted from a somewhat narrow early emphasis on the concepts of 'absolute' and 'relative' poverty to a more critical and up-to-date notion of social exclusion and participation. In addition, research has usefully highlighted links between poverty and physical and mental ill-health (Blackburn, 1992).

There has also been useful research focusing on social workers' professional ambivalence in providing welfare rights advice and advocacy (Fimister, 1986). However, such studies have a largely British perspective, with practitioners mainly being located within local authorities in England and Wales rather than in the integrated health and social services established in Northern Ireland. Significant research has, in addition, focused on the concept of change and leadership within social work and health service organisations (Stewart, 1989; Covey, 1996). This has offered useful pointers to the social worker who wishes to embrace a more radical agenda in the area of poverty and welfare rights. On the other hand, literature and research on the issue of poverty, and on the role of welfare rights in social work, has a number of limitations. For example, recent debates about the concept of an 'underclass' – often characterised by a range of negative social and behavioural traits – appears to have gained significant governmental and media support. Moreover, the focus within much of the research on the need for welfare rights advocacy within the social work profession has obscured the reality of much social work within the multi-disciplinary framework. The blurring of professional boundaries – between social workers and nurses in multi-disciplinary teams – has major implications for social workers' traditional involvement in benefits advice and financial assessments. This is an area that has attracted little research to date.

Finally, while there has been considerable interest, and official endorsement, in the concept of partnership between the statutory and voluntary sector in the provision of health and social care, little research has been undertaken into the potential of partnership initiatives in the welfare rights field.

Welfare rights as a policy issue

Nationally, there has been widespread debate about the nature of poverty, and the financial needs of disabled people. The Government has, in recent years, signalled increasing concern at the apparent spiralling of social security costs in meeting the needs of claimants on disability benefits. This has prompted a wide-ranging and controversial review of benefits such as Incapacity Benefit and Disability Living Allowance, and the plans to reduce entitlement to sickness and disability-related benefits contained in the Welfare and Reform and Pensions Bill. It has also given rise to initiatives such as the New Deal for the disabled, aiming to move claimants off benefits and welfare dependency and into the workplace.

Within Northern Ireland, the Health and Social Services Boards and Trusts have experienced growing demands and pressures on their budgets and services, especially since the introduction of the community care reforms in the early 1990s. Front-line staff have increasingly been drawn into undertaking financial assessments of those requiring community care services, and Trusts have been looking for guidance on how to formulate new charging policies for those needing domiciliary services such as home help. This, in turn, has raised the question of whether service users – many of whom are on benefit – can afford to meet the cost of new charges. In this context, there have been calls for a welfare rights strategy that would help ensure that clients, who are asked to pay for services, are receiving their full benefit entitlements.

However, for many social workers and healthcare professionals working in the statutory sector, the issue of poverty and welfare rights has proved especially challenging. Many practitioners have acknowledged that they lack the skills and training to allow them to give adequate benefits advice (Fimister, 1986). As Walker and Walker (1998, p 55) have stressed:

> The majority of social work service users are poor, yet poverty as an issue is

> too often marginalised in social work training, even though it is a greater cause of social exclusion than are 'race' and 'gender', with which it also overlaps.

Again, many benefit specialists working in the voluntary sector have considerable technical expertise in social security matters. However, they have little meaningful contact with statutory sector staff who are working on a daily basis with the most vulnerable. The potential for a more effective partnership – to alleviate the impact of poverty – has not been fully realised.

For many service users, the experience of living on social security and the need to secure sufficient benefit entitlements have been fraught with difficulty. The limited research undertaken in this area suggests that claimants with mental health needs experience particular problems when trying to access key benefits, or when attempting to obtain appropriate advice when challenging official decisions (Social Security Advisory Committee Report, 1996). This uncertainty and confusion has been compounded by official reviews and questioning of disabled people's benefits entitlement through the Benefits Integrity Project and New Deal initiative.

The challenge for social work

In the light of the above, how can social work, particularly in the field of mental health, address the issues of poverty and inequality? Can social workers in mental health teams, operating within a tradition of individual casework and confronted by medical models of client pathology, embrace a more radical and strategic approach when combating the material deprivation that faces so many of their clients? To address this question the remaining part of this paper will be structured as follows.

First, the author focuses on social workers' motivation and capacity to respond to the financial needs of service users. As social work has appeared to move from an earlier focus during the 1970s on 'radical' and anti-oppressive practice to its current preoccupation with 'technocratic' efficiency (with its emphasis on productivity and measurement of outcomes), the author seeks to test whether current practices avoid the wider issues of poverty and economic injustice. As Walker and Walker have argued (p 55):

> The pressures of recent years to reduce the role of the welfare state, for both ideological and financial reasons, have made it much more likely that vulnerable people will find themselves in need – in this climate it is particularly important for those working with the poor to look beyond individual hardship, and sometimes inadequacy, to the structural factors which exclude the poor from sharing in the life-styles of the wider society.

In the context of these shifting priorities within social work, the author aims to explore an alternative approach in which the issues of poverty and welfare rights are more directly addressed. For some observers (Banks, 1995) such an approach cannot ignore the issue of public or collective welfare. Here the social worker has a 'responsibility to challenge oppression and to work for changes in agency policy and in society' (p 13). Through a discussion of a number of research and training initiatives undertaken by the author in the field of welfare rights for people with mental health needs, this paper attempts to map out a more challenging role for social workers and their colleagues in multi-disciplinary teams in Northern Ireland.

A second strand of this discussion is to explore the potential for greater collaboration with, and mutual respect between, different disciplines involved with service users who have benefits problems. To date, most research undertaken in Britain has concentrated on the capacity of social workers as a distinct profession to respond to the needs of the vulnerable poor (Fimister). However, in the field of mental health, particularly within integrated health and social services in Northern Ireland, social workers are often located within multi-disciplinary teams. Here all front-line staff, whether from social work or nursing backgrounds, may have to perform a 'key worker' role. In this situation no individual discipline has the monopoly in benefits advice or advocacy. Consequently, attention needs to focus on the ways in which an integrated approach can be developed by professionals who hope to alleviate the material deprivation that faces many users of mental health services.

A third and final element to the discussion, and one that is particularly relevant in Northern Ireland, is the examination of the potential for closer partnership arrangements between mental health professionals in the statutory sector and staff within voluntary bodies when responding to poverty.

Implicit within all these dimensions is the challenge facing social workers who wish to take a leadership role during times of change. Whether through research, training, or influencing policy, the field of welfare rights provides a golden opportunity for modern social work to reassert its traditional concerns with the broader issues of poverty, equality and anti-oppressive practice.

The research and training initiative

It is these issues forming the backdrop to the research and training initiative that the author examined during 1998 and 1999 within the Sperrin Lakeland Health and Social Services Trust. The overall aim of the project was to promote a welfare rights strategy in the Trust. Initially, the strategy focused on mental health services. In order to develop the strategy, two objectives were identified.

The first was to carry out a needs analysis by surveying mental health professionals and voluntary sector benefits advisers. The surveys attempted to identify the key issues that would have to be addressed in order for a welfare rights strategy to be effective. The second objective was more action-orientated: it was to establish a benefits training programme for staff who are frequently required to advise vulnerable clients in financial difficulty. Ultimately, the broader aim of the project – to promote a comprehensive welfare rights strategy within the Trust – would be dependent on the success of these two objectives.

In terms of methodology the project had three elements. The first consisted of a survey, using structured questionnaires, of people with identified mental health needs, who were seeking advice from a Citizens Advice Bureau (CAB) concerning their benefits and finances. The focus of the survey was the experiences of CAB customers facing deprivation and mental ill-health. It also aimed to explore the views of those benefit advisers who were trying to assist them. Forty-one CAB customers, with identified mental health needs, were interviewed over a two-month period. CAB advisers judged a case to have a mental health dimension on the basis of information (about mental health needs) within a customer's benefit claim or appeal papers (for example, medical evidence from a doctor or psychiatrist). The questionnaire asked CAB staff, following their interviews, to indicate the type of benefit issue facing their clients; to find out whether they were in contact with the local community mental health team; and if so, to note whether a key worker from the team was currently assisting with the benefits problem. The questionnaire also asked advisers to state whether such involvement by the mental health team had been useful in resolving their clients' benefits problems. While the sample selected was limited to one CAB, it represented a total population of those customers with identified mental health needs who had approached the bureau for help over the two-month period.

The second element of the project comprised a survey of the views of twenty-six key workers – mainly social workers and psychiatric nurses – who worked in two community mental health teams. Through structured questionnaires the survey aimed to assess practitioners' attitudes towards providing benefits advice and advocacy as well as gauging their interest in working more closely with benefits specialists in the voluntary sector. The survey also asked key workers about the type of training and in-service support they felt they would need in order to provide effective advice and advocacy. The choice of a structured questionnaire was largely dictated by the limitations of time: it would not have been possible to carry out face-to-face interviews with twenty-six staff from the two teams. Nevertheless, the response rate was relatively high: 80 per cent of staff responded from the author's own team, and 50 per cent completed questionnaires from the other mental health team.

The third element of the project consisted of a benefits training programme for practitioners from different disciplines, for example social workers and nurses and from various programmes of care such as mental health, elderly and health care services. During 1998 and 1999 two benefits training programmes were run. The first included basic benefits training and was provided to staff directly by the author under the auspices of the social services training team. The second, more advanced course, was run by the Law Centre (NI). In all, 41 staff participated in the two courses.

In many respects the three elements of the project were complementary. While the two surveys identified key issues and helped to outline an agenda for action, the benefits training initiative gave practical expression to calls – from service users, practitioners and advisers alike – for a more effective welfare rights strategy within the Trust. The author was aware that the reliability of the findings could be hampered as colleagues might be tempted to provide answers they believed he would wish to hear. However, the use of anonymous questionnaires, as well as independent evaluation (through the social services training team) of the benefits training, helped to reduce the risk of bias.

Findings

Survey of CAB clients

- The scope of their problems was extensive: difficulties in obtaining benefits, social security appeals, debt, as well as legal, employment, and housing matters.
- They were, in the main, seeking help with claims for, or appeals over, a range of disability-related benefits, such as Disability Living Allowance (54%), Incapacity Benefit (41%), and Community Care Grants (15%).
- Over half (58%) had no contact with statutory mental health services.
- Of those in touch with statutory services, the majority (58%) reported that the help they received from key workers with benefit problems had been useful.
- CAB advisers reported that, in 66% of cases surveyed, a twin approach by voluntary and statutory sector professionals had been more effective in resolving their clients' benefits or financial difficulties.
- The issue of benefits entitlement and the need for effective advocacy both from advisers in the voluntary sector and key workers in the statutory services, was highlighted.

Survey of key workers in two community mental health teams

- A majority of staff (87%) expressed a clear commitment to the need to help clients with benefits or financial problems
- Most professionals (73%) stated that they needed additional training in benefits.

- A majority of staff (58%) were particularly interested in outreach-based welfare rights initiatives such as 'benefits surgeries' in psychiatric hospital or day centres.
- Most practitioners (87%) saw a need for closer working links with voluntary sector benefits advisers when dealing with clients who had both financial as well as mental health needs.

The key finding arising out of this survey was that staff working with vulnerable clients in financial difficulty did not feel sufficiently equipped or skilled to provide effective welfare rights advice or support. This points to the need for a welfare rights strategy that enhances practitioners' skills in benefits advice and advocacy on the one hand and promotes a closer working partnership with the voluntary sector on the other.

The benefits training initiative

The training programmes generated a number of issues:

- There was, initially, some reluctance among senior managers to run separate benefits courses for different disciplines within the mental health team, as had originally been proposed by the author. Such an approach, they argued, could be divisive and contrary to the ethos of multi-disciplinary team-work.
- However, this problem was resolved when staff were permitted to choose the courses that they felt most suited their needs. There was a general tendency for social workers to opt for advanced level benefits training, and for nurses to select the basic benefits programme.
- There was a consensus among most key workers that benefits training – at whatever level – was highly relevant to their day-to-day work. In addition, many staff agreed that training would need to be ongoing in order for practitioners to remain up-to-date.

For staff working with vulnerable clients training is judged to be the key to effective benefits advice and advocacy. While different disciplines appeared to require differing levels of benefits training, the social services training team, who evaluated the course, concluded that 'the consensus of feed-back received was that the training proved worthwhile and beneficial – with clear statements about future training needs'.

Conclusions and recommendations

How do these findings help us to redefine a role for social workers, in the field of mental health, at the close of the 1990s?

First, the findings from the surveys, and the outcome of the training initiative, help to relocate the issue of poverty and welfare rights within the social work agenda. Clearly, an individualistic casework approach – focusing largely on a client's behaviour or personal deficits – will miss a key area of their daily experience, namely their financial or material circumstances.

Second, it is evident that social workers are unlikely to bring about significant change, or a real improvement in their clients' lives, through a half-hearted or *ad hoc* approach to benefits advice and advocacy. Rather, a strategic approach that takes account of the expressed needs of both service users and practitioners on the one hand, and commands the support of senior managers on the other, is essential. This must be underpinned by ongoing training at all levels for staff who have front-line contact with vulnerable clients in financial need. Any ambivalence among social work staff, or within other disciplines, about the value of welfare rights should become a thing of the past.

Third, a welfare rights strategy needs to be proactive and innovative. The setting-up of benefits surgeries where clients can get advice and support in convenient locations, or during periods when their benefits are likely to be disrupted, for example in hospital, should be actively pursued.

Fourth, social workers who are working in a multi-disciplinary setting can no longer regard benefits advice as the preserve of their own discipline. While other professions, such as nursing, may have yet to embrace the issue of poverty or welfare rights as whole-heartedly as many social workers, the reality of multi-disciplinary team-work, especially in the field of mental health, means that no key workers can simply ignore their clients' material well-being. It must be recognised that some technical expertise about benefits is now a prerequisite for resolving the increasingly complex social security problems that face many service users. For social workers, moreover, a collaborative approach over welfare rights – in which practitioners work productively with other disciplines or outside agencies – is already part of an established tradition of networking.

Finally, both the research and training initiatives have demonstrated the importance of leadership and innovation within present day social work. True, the training programmes did require a level of backing from senior managers. However, the participation of staff in mapping out their own training needs and their expressed interest in the wider issues of poverty during training sessions, demonstrated that this was not simply a hierarchical or top-down initiative. As Covey (1996) has pointed out, positive change is unlikely to occur unless the initiator prepares and nurtures the ground first. Moreover, the area of welfare rights can provide the social worker with an ideal opportunity to take a more collegiate role within the multi-disciplinary setting. The author's experience of providing benefits training to a multi-disciplinary group has highlighted some of the key qualities that will be needed increasingly in modern social work. As Hawkins and Shohet (1996) have noted, such training events offer good opportunities for non-hierarchical group supervision – where the facilitator acts as 'expert technician, colleague and leader'.

Postscript

Following the research and training initiatives outlined above, the Sperrin Lakeland Trust's Mental Health and Elderly Services Directorate has agreed on the need for benefits training to be ongoing – particularly in the light of the social security changes that will follow government legislation on sickness and disability benefits, and after the introduction of the New Deal for disabled people. The Trust has also fostered closer links with the CAB, setting up, for example, a pilot benefits surgery run by CAB staff at the admission wards of the psychiatric hospital. These positive steps demonstrate the Trust's recognition of the importance of the financial well-being of service users, and of the value of a strategic welfare rights approach in tackling poverty. Such initiatives also highlight the opportunity, open to all social workers, to reassert their traditional concerns and values and, in doing so, to move beyond the profession's current preoccupation with technocratic efficiency – setting social work a radical and dynamic agenda at the start of the twenty-first century.

References

Banks, S. (1995) *Ethics and Values in Social Work*, London: Macmillan

Blackburn, C. (1992) *Poverty and Health: Working With Families*, Buckingham: Open University

Covey, R. (1996) *Principle-Centred Leadership*, London: Simon & Schuster

Fimister, G. (1986) *Welfare Rights in Social Services*, London: Macmillan Education

Hawkins, P. and Shohet, R. (1996) *Supervision in the Helping Professions*, Buckingham: Open University

Social Security Advisory Committee (1996) *Health: Report on the SSAC Workshop*, London: HMSO

Stewart, R. (1989) *Leading in the NHS: A Practical Guide*, London: Macmillan

Viney, A. (1999) 'Slipping Through the Safety Net: Towards a Welfare Rights Strategy in Mental Health', Unpublished dissertation, University of Ulster

Walker, C. and Walker, A. (1998) 'Social Policy and Social Work', in Adams, R., Dominelli, L. and Payne, M. (eds.) *Social Work – Themes, Issues and Current Debates*, London: Macmillan

5 Suspected and convicted sex offenders: the challenge for social work practice

Marcella Leonard

Introduction

There has been a significant amount of research carried out on sex offenders, looking at their *modus operandi* and trying to identify theories which can help to explain their behaviour. However, most of this research has been based on offenders in America or in England with little known about sex offending in Northern Ireland. This research was an attempt to gain a regional perspective by developing a profile of the offenders referred to the Programme for Prevention of Sexual Abuse (PPSA). The PPSA is a community-based programme established in 1994 by the Western Health & Social Services Board (WHSSB) to work with convicted sex offenders. The rationale for the research emanated from the observation that the type of individual being referred to the programme did not conform to a perceived, taken-for-granted profile. In other words, offenders did not appear to fit the stereotype of isolated, disconnected social outcasts. Rather, they appeared to have maintained their familial and social contacts. To test this observation, attempts were made to collate a picture of these individuals in relation to their social, marital and employment circumstances as well as the nature of their sexual offending including their abuse history. At the outset, it was believed that this information would have an important bearing on service planning and delivery; that is, it would have direct implications for assessment, treatment and the management of offenders in the community.

Outline of relevant literature

There are difficulties conducting a literature review of this area because of the problematic issue of defining what constitutes sexual molestation. Clearly, there is a danger of creating an overly simplistic definition of what, on the face of it, is a heterogeneous group of behaviours and cognitions. No two sex offenders are the same but research has begun to identify similar traits, such as how offenders access the child without detection, their grooming of the child, their family and significant others, and the role of fantasy. Consequently, rather than trying to categorise offenders, research has tended to concentrate on trying to understand their behaviour and the findings have had an important bearing on treatment strategies. It is important to bear in mind, though, that any research has to contend with individuals who strive, as part of their *modus operandi*, to deny, minimise and blame others or their circumstances for their offending. Nevertheless, a comprehensive body of theory has been developed. This ranges from a biological theory highlighted by authors such as Bradford (1985), Goodman (1987), Henry (1987) and Berlin (1989), who believe that offenders are not bad but ill. In contrast, psychodynamic theory (Bender and Blau, 1937) posits that victims are ready participants and active initiators of an incestuous relationship. Alternatively, the family dysfunctions model (Mrazek and Bentovim, 1981; de Young, 1982; Alexander, 1985) suggests that incest has been the result of family dysfunction and that the perpetrator utilises incest to reduce tension in order to maintain balance within the family. Behavioural theory can be contrasted with all of these approaches because it views sexual offending as a learned behaviour. It is now commonly accepted, however, that there are limitations to these single factor models, particularly given the complexity of the phenomenon. As Morrison *et al.* (1994) observe:

> The limitations of single factor theories have resulted in several multi-factorial models being proposed which, whilst not perfect, have proved more helpful in understanding the development of deviant sexual behaviour.

In line with this consensus, Finkelhor (1984) has identified four conditions which must co-exist to enable the offender to move beyond fantasy and carry out sexual acts on children. First, the offender has to have the motivation to abuse and an emotional congruence with children. Second, he (*sic*) must have overcome internal inhibitors to abuse. Third, he must have identified and created situations where abuse can occur and overcome any external obstacles. Last, he must overcome the child's resistance.

However, in acknowledging the range of literature on the complexities of this client group, it is clear that there is a significant gap in our information regarding the offender's personal, situational and demographic characteristics (particularly within Northern Ireland). Importantly, if it were available, this information would have a direct bearing not only on theory-building in this fraught area, but more pertinently on strategies directed to risk assessment and management.

Context of practice

In establishing the PPSA it was hypothesised that the majority of the referrals would include convicted sex offenders who were living apart from their families, especially if there were under-age children living in the home. However, as the programme developed this hypothesis was not substantiated (offenders seemed rather to maintain their familial connections) and this led to the adoption of a biopsychosocial model incorporating Finkelhor's four-factor model: offenders are made to focus on all parts of their lives, not just the offence. In other words, it is an holistic model.

In keeping with this holistic stance, an integral part of this programme is that the offender's spouse (or significant others in the offender's life) also has to attend for assessment. The PPSA acknowledges that sexual abuse affects the whole system in which it takes place regardless of whether it is intra- or extra-familial. Therefore, only to work with the victim – and possibly the perpetrator – means the whole abusive environment created by the perpetrator goes unchallenged.

The fact that the programme engaged spouses and significant others meant that a lot of information regarding the background of these abusive environments came to light. Also, the fact the PPSA has an open referral system meant that for the first time, there was an identified programme for unconvicted sex offenders. In fact, the programme began to have a client base significantly different to the one initially envisaged. The perception that a fundamentally different cohort was being referred to the programme led the author to instigate this research.

Methodology

Given that the PPSA was established in October 1994, it was decided to carry out a retrospective analysis of all referrals since its inception (the research period ran from October 1994 to October 1997). It identified 101 individuals whose characteristics could be collated and analysed. The criterion for inclusion was that the person had to have at least three months contact with the programme to ensure that the information needed was available. In order to protect the identity of the research sample no names, addresses or dates of birth were used and each client had a research number unrelated to any of their programme records. This procedure was given approval by the ethical committee of the Sperrin Lakeland Health and Social Services Trust. The tool used for the research was a questionnaire in which each question had several answer options. The format was then copied to a research database for analysis.

The questionnaire was piloted on ten clients by the author and, after some changes to the format, was then used with the sample. The questionnaire was completed using the data from case-notes either completed by the author or the key worker following individual interviews. It had seven main areas – subdivided into relevant sections – comprising referral details, offence details, social history, victim details, history, psychometric tests, and appointment details. For the purpose of this paper I will draw on selected findings from these areas which are most relevant to social work policy and practice.

Results and outcomes

Figure 5.1 Legal status at time of referral

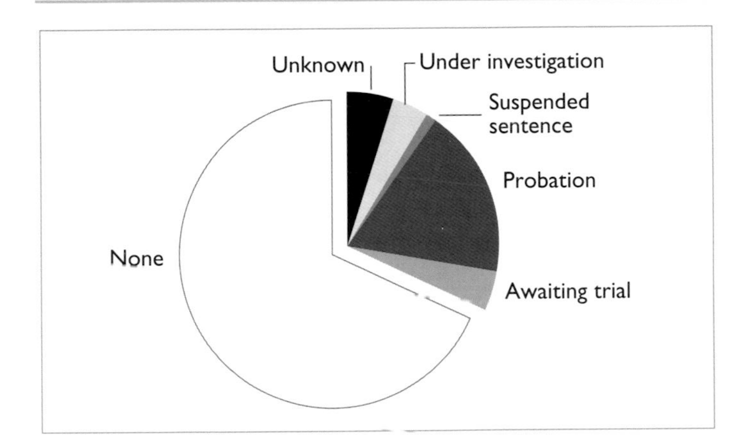

Of the sample of 101, 69 were referred to the programme under no legal sanction for their offences. Other studies point to a poor voluntary uptake of similar programmes (Sgori, 1982). However, in this study individuals attended at the insistence of social services, family members or sometimes the victim; clearly these pressures can be as effective as legal sanctions. The figures also show that many sex offenders are unconvicted and so are *de facto* 'law-abiding citizens' who do not have to declare their abusive behaviours on an application form. It is also notable that 40 per cent of referrals were from childcare teams who apparently are having to work increasingly with this population and face difficulties of establishing a professional mandate with them.

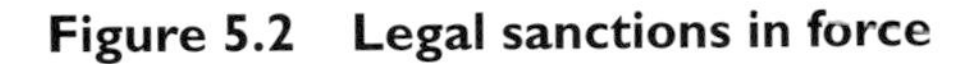

Figure 5.2 Legal sanctions in force

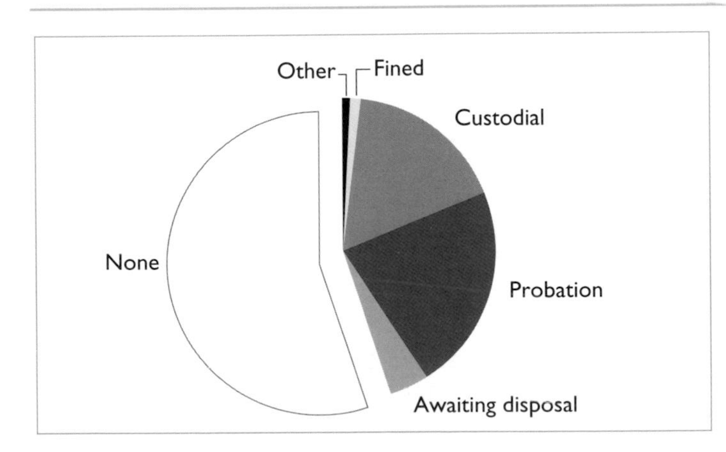

The findings indicate that 55 per cent of the sample group were attending the programme under no conviction for their offences. They also highlight that 57 of the original sample group (56%) legally had no previous sexual offences yet 35 per cent admitted to making their first inappropriate sexual touch before the age of 20. A study by Abel *et al.* (1985) on 411 sex offenders demonstrated that 58 per cent of them admitted to the onset of deviant behaviour in adolescence. Also of significance was the finding that 57 clients had no previous sexual conviction and 23 had no previous non-sexual conviction: to society at large they were 'law-abiding' individuals.

Figure 5.3 Marital status of clients on referral

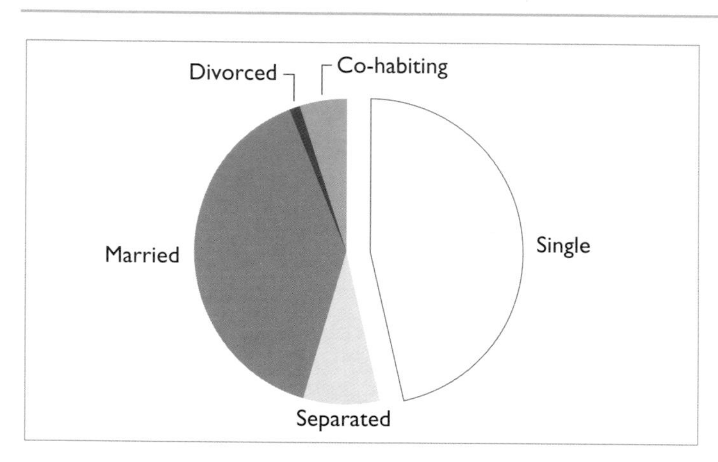

Figure 5.4 Residence at time of referral

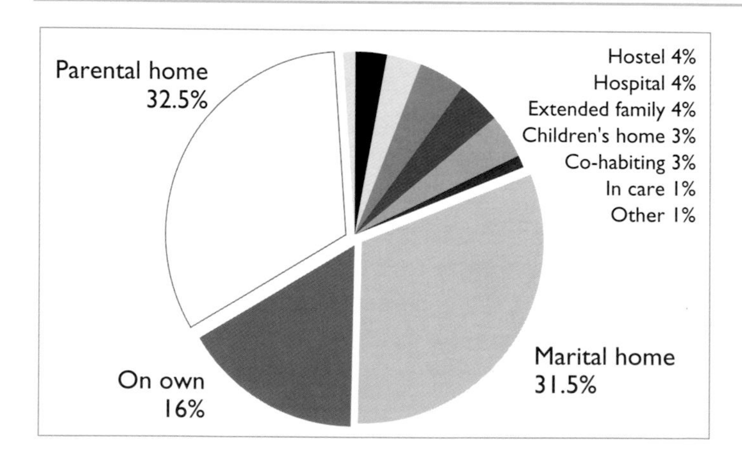

Figures 5.3 and 5.4 show the reality of the social circumstances of the sample group. Convicted or not, they have admitted to serious sexual offences against

children, yet they are still living as part of their families, whether marital or extended. As Figure 5.3 shows, 54 per cent were married, separated or in an adult relationship while they attended the programme. In the case of those separated this was usually due to social services' involvement, even though the spouse was still a part of the offender's life. Abel *et al.*, in a similar study of non-incarcerated offenders, found that 47 per cent were single, 29 per cent married and the remaining 24 per cent had a relationship with an adult at some stage. Figure 5.4 highlights the reality that the sample group lived in social situations where children were also present and even those in caring institutions mixed with vulnerable people.

Figure 5.5 Relationship of offender to victim

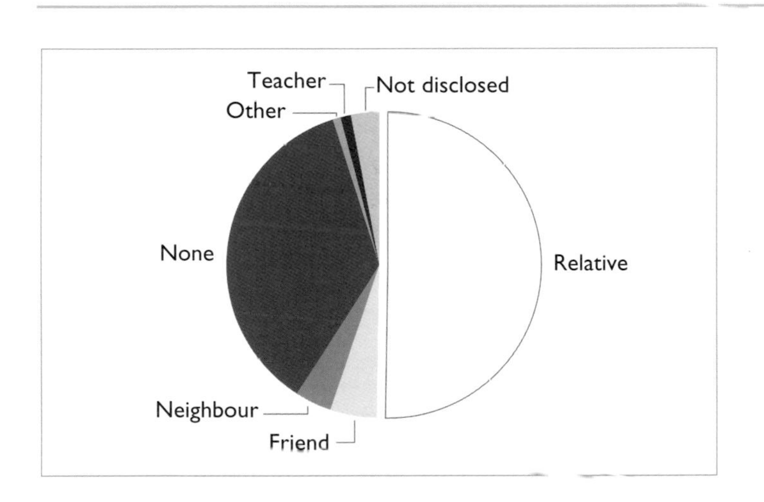

These findings highlight that the cohort, in the main, usually abused someone they were either related to or knew very well. This challenges the 'stranger–danger' concept which is often taught to children by parents or society at large. The fact that the abuser is possibly daddy, granda or brother makes it hard for the victim to disclose, and harder still to take those disclosures to social services and ultimately the court. It is more difficult for the victim and often the other family members to ostracise a family member than a stranger, so offenders often remain in the family unit. Alarmingly, 41 per cent of the offenders disclosed that they had been sexually abused and of this group 28 per cent stated that the abuse was by a relative or someone with whom their family had a relationship or friendship.

Implications for practice

In looking at the implications of this research for social work practice, it is first of all useful to turn to the statement by Herman (1990) that 'the most striking characteristic of sex offenders, from a diagnostic standpoint, is their apparent normality'. Historically, the image that the public at large had of sex offenders was that they were monsters – 'dirty old men' that were different to everyone else. Contrary to those perceptions the findings illustrated above highlights that these men (*sic*) are in the main ordinary and, whether they have had a conviction or not, are still very much part of our communities: they are continuing to live in family situations with – and this does present a challenge to social work – family support. Previously, it was rare for a convicted sex offender to live with the family. However, this appears to be changing, due perhaps to the fact that the spouse, for whatever reasons, wants to maintain a relationship with the offender. In addition, the poor conviction rates after disclosures of abuse lead, in many instances, to victims feeling ambivalent about police intervention.

A second observation suggests that there is a need for social workers to stand back and take a non-judgmental view of the offender's spouse or significant others in the offender's life. The offender has committed the offences; the child has become a victim, but within the system there are also people who have been abused by the offender, albeit in different ways. When an allegation occurs, the procedural process of Joint Protocol has to take place, but within the process there always appears to be an expectation that the spouse will respond appropriately; that is, actively protect the child and extricate the offender. However, this often creates an unhelpful ambivalence for the spouse, particularly if she does not want to separate from her partner. Moreover, if the victim is not able to insist on the offender's removal, it can appear that the victim also wants him to remain at home. Understandably, social services often require the offender to leave the home in order to prevent repeated victimisation. However, if the offender moves in with the extended family, as highlighted earlier, he may continue to have access to children even if they do not include the original victim. Alongside this is the difficulty that if extended family members are not assessed on their understanding of the offender's risk to others, and educated in how to become effective external monitors of his behaviour, then treatment is likely to be only partially successful.

The model of work within PPSA required spouses and significant others to attend for assessment, which provided insights into their thoughts and feelings. Spouses often refer to the experience of the disclosure of abuse, whether intra- or extra-familial, as similar to a death taking place: they describe the experience in terms of a grieving process like the one identified by Kubler-Ross (1969). Therefore, at a time when social workers need them to be assertive, independent and rational, spouses may be in the denial stage of grief, thinking it is not possible that the man they married, loved and were happy with is now a child-abuser. Yet spouses need to be there in order to protect the children – a difficult balance but one which must be achieved. Many families experiencing abuse will therefore want to remain intact, and social workers must accept this reality.

Third, there is a need to include the spouse in the assessment process to enable the worker to understand fully the environment in which the abuse took place. To achieve this, the social worker must acknowledge and identify with the spouse's feelings and then encourage her in attending for assessment. She must see that this is a vital part of the process if she wants her partner re-integrated into the home. Thus, acknowledgement by child protection workers that sex offenders are often married or living with a partner (54 per cent of the sample), and that their partners may want to remain with them, can lay the foundation for an effective assessment and treatment. Intervention is also more effective if the couple can be open about their wish to remain together as it prevents the pretence of separate living arrangements to placate social services.

This requires child protection professionals to examine why they automatically demand that offenders remove themselves when it might be better if they lived with an informed rather than an uninformed supervisor. Greater reflection on this point will assist those supervising the offender (for example, the Probation Officer) as O'Rourke highlights (see chapter six). Critically, social workers need to reassure spouses that they can work in partnership with them even though the spouse might wish to remain in a relationship with the offender. That said, spouses must ensure that they adhere to the stance that the child's welfare is of paramount importance.

Figure 5.4 also shows that it is important to educate spouses in the dynamics of the abuse so that they can become effective protectors and monitors. Thus, the challenge is to work with the complete system, taking account of where the abuse took place. To leave out an approach to significant others results in a partial (and an insensitive) service. Equally, in order for the offender to abuse, grooming has invariably occurred; it is important to acknowledge that spouses may also be victims of this grooming process. It is vital that all victims are educated in how this process develops, otherwise recovery work may be undermined by a spouse who still believes her husband's excuses.

Fourth, as Figures 5.1 and 5.2 highlight, a growing number of unconvicted sex offenders are coming to the attention of social services and programmes like PPSA. These findings raise the question of who is responsible for supervising unconvicted offenders. Conviction usually brings with it legal constraints which can be utilised to encourage an offender and spouse to abide by the requests of social services. However, with the unconvicted offender, expedience demands the engagement of the offender's spouse as the only external supervising person available. For this partnership approach to work successfully there needs to be an acceptance of the time needed to work with spouses who are trying to come to terms with events. The time constraints on social workers caught up in procedural imperatives mean that protocols and procedures do not allow much flexibility. Yet what flexibility there is, if used effectively, can create a more protective, questioning and assertive mother or partner.

For the future it is vital to review the current strategy for managing sex offenders in the community. We need always to remember the degree of duplicity involved in committing acts of sexual molestation against children. Working with the whole system might prove to be an important way of challenging this duplicity.

References

Abel, G.G., Mittelman, M.S., and Becker, J.V. (1985) 'Sexual Offenders: Results of assessment and recommendations for treatment' in Salter, A.C. (1995) *Transforming Trauma, A Guide to Understanding and Treating Adult Survivors of Child Sexual Abuse*, California: Sage Publications

Alexander, P.C. (1985) 'A Systems Theory Conceptualization of Incest', *Family Process*, 24, 79–87

Bender, L. and Blau, A. (1937) 'The Reaction of Children to Sexual Relations with Adults', *American Journal of Orthopsychiatry*, 7, 500–18

Finkelhor, D. (1984) *Child sexual abuse: new theory and research*, New York: Free Press

Goodman, R.E. (1987) 'Genetic and Hormonal Factors in Human Sexuality: Evolutionary and Developmental Perspectives', in Wilson, G.D. (ed.) *Variant Sexuality: Research and Theory*, Baltimore, MD: John Hopkins University

Herman, J.L. (1990) 'Sex Offenders: A Feminist Perspective', in Marshall, W.L, Laws, D.R. and Barbaree, H.E. (eds.) *Handbook of Sexual Assault: Issues, Theories and Treatment of the Offender*, New York: Plenum

Kubler-Ross, E. (1969) *On death and dying*, New York: Macmillan

Morrison, T., Erooga, M. and Beckett, R. (1994) *Sexual Offending Against Children: Assessment and Treatment of Male Abusers*, London: Routledge

Mrazek, P.B., and Bentovim, A. (1981) 'Incest and the dysfunctional family system', in Mrazek, P.B. and Kempe, C.H. (eds.) *Sexually abused children and their families*, New York: Pergamon

Sgori, S. (1982) *Handbook of Clinical Intervention in Child Sexual Abuse*, Lexington, MA: Lexington Books

de Young (1982) *The Sexual Victimization of Children*, Jefferson, NC: McFarland

6 Supervising sex offenders in our communities: are we able to respond effectively?

Marian O'Rourke

Introduction

Are we, within the fields of criminal justice and child protection, equipped to manage sex offenders in the community? This is an emotive and controversial question. In this chapter I will explore some of the literature and research that guides and informs policy and practice in relation to the supervision of sex offenders in our communities. Additionally, I will identify particular gaps in practice and describe an ethos of change that led the Probation Board in Northern Ireland (PBNI) to develop a Manual of Guidance for their staff who had the responsibility of supervising sex offenders in the community. As a key contributor to the manual, I will outline its content and practical application. Finally, I will consider significant developments in policy and practice within this field of work that will have direct implications for the review and development of the manual. In doing so, I hope to have informed the reader about the structures that are in place and the dilemmas that remain for criminal justice and child protection social work in the task of managing sex offenders in the community.

Managing sex offenders in the community – what the literature and the legislation tell us

Those who are experienced in working with sexual abuse agree that it should treated as a crime and managed within the criminal justice system (Morrison, 1994; Becker and Kaplin, 1988; Salter, 1998). This approach has two benefits: the perpetrator is held accountable for his actions; and a system of monitoring and supervision can be in place should he remain in or return to the community. In some instances it also creates the opportunity for the offender to address his abusive behaviour in a programme of treatment.

However, for some victims, particularly those of intra-familial abuse, the criminal justice system is not a route they wish to travel. For them it is not about punishment but about wanting the abuse to stop. The offender must be denied the opportunity to continue his abusive behaviour if circumstances permit him to remain within a family network (see chapter five). Whatever premise one takes, the common ground is that the behaviour must be controlled. This must therefore be the basis for intervention with all sex offenders, whether within the criminal justice system or in other programmes of care.

Based on sound risk assessment, programmes in the community must address two areas of concern: ameliorating the individual offender's behaviour; and the protection of others. The focus of intervention for those at high risk of re-offending must therefore include treatment and supervision. To lock up or supervise the offender for a period of time may address the issue of access to potential victims but does nothing to change the offender's thinking in relation to his behaviour. To ensure attendance at a treatment programme may address the offender's understanding of his behaviour but does nothing to monitor whether or not change is taking place within his lifestyle. An effective response to the management of sex offenders in the community clearly requires both aspects of the problem to be addressed. Morrison (p 28) tells us that 'the management of offenders requires a co-ordinated response involving criminal justice and child protection agencies'.

Roberts (1991), in his review of what works with serious and persistent offenders in any category, proposes that there is a need for four levels of intervention:

- specific work on offending behaviours
- work on associated behaviours
- addressing current problems and stress factors
- community re-integration.

Roberts' findings apply equally to sex offenders. The reasons for sexual abuse are complex and multi-causal. Tomison (1995) advises that despite a range of research no consistent profile has emerged beyond the fact that most sex offenders are men. Since sex offenders are not a homogeneous group no single response is adequate; moreover, no one discipline has the breadth or depth to respond alone. The harm created by such offenders is widespread and often long-lasting. The response to managing sex offenders must therefore be multi-faceted, taking account of victim, perpetrator, the family of both, other potential victims, and the community context.

Monitoring and supervising sex offenders in the community, along with treatment interventions, directly contribute to the protection of the public and potential victims. The process of supervision must therefore be focused on child and public protection. Morrison reminds us that such a focus is recent in origin. Between 1983 and 1987 there was an 800 per cent increase in the registration of sexually-abused children. In that same period prosecutions for sexual abuse rose only by 17 per cent (p 26):

> In other words, whilst the professional community was facing an explosion of demand to protect and care for the victims of sexual abuse, the criminal

justice system appeared to be ineffective in identifying and controlling offenders.

It is surely a compelling and embarrassing indictment of our society that it has taken until the latter years of the twentieth century to produce a co-ordinated response from all agencies to the sexual abuse of children. However, a range of legislation, policy and procedures has been introduced in recent years, in an attempt to reduce the gaps in this field and this must surely be welcomed. Some developments have addressed the needs of victims while others have provided stronger powers in responding to the offender.

Victims can now give evidence in court by video link from another room. Offenders can be supervised on licence after serving a prison sentence under Article 26 of the Criminal Justice Order (NI) 1996. A probation officer supervises the licence and the process is therefore subject to PBNI's inter-agency child protection procedures. Courts can also combine sentences, most notably custody probation orders, also under the new powers of the 1996 Order. This ensures that the offender will spend a period of time in custody and be supervised in the community on release; he can also be mandated to attend treatment programmes as a condition of the supervision. Treatment programmes are also available in prisons, but attendance there is voluntary. The Sex Offenders Act 1997 now requires convicted sex offenders to register with the police for varying periods of time determined by the nature of the sentence imposed.

Whilst all of the changes in legislation, policy and procedures recognise and allow for more detailed monitoring of the offender in the community, it was clear from a practice perspective that further guidance was required for staff before they could feel both confident and competent to take on this high profile task. In chapter seven, Smyth tells us that to ensure effective implementation of change, the development of practice knowledge, skill and competence is as crucial as organisational development. If supervision in the community is to be effective all agencies must work together to empower staff in the development of the necessary knowledge and skills. All relevant agencies must own the process. Morrison (p 30) concluded that practice guidelines have in the past been underdeveloped, leading to a situation where:

> managers are unable to exercise accountability, and clients, workers and agencies are vulnerable if complaints are made, or practice is thought to be unsatisfactory. It also hinders the development of consistency and accountability.

To summarise, there are a number of key messages emerging from a review of current practice in this area:

- Sexual abuse causes harm to the victim and those close to him or her.
- Offenders must be held accountable for their behaviour and this issue is best managed within the criminal justice and social care structures.
- Intervention must incorporate both treatment and supervision if an effective and comprehensive programme of management in the community is to be put in place.
- Community education must be embraced by all agencies already involved in this field of work, as well as other relevant bodies coming on stream. Child protection and protection of the public must be regarded as public health issues.

These imperatives require clear and focused guidance. However, before the manual is described, it is important first to examine the contextual factors shaping its development.

Context of practice

The task of managing sex offenders within our communities necessitates protecting the innocent from harm, educating the public, taking care of the victims, and dealing with the perpetrator in a way that will not prejudice his rights as a human being but controls and changes his behaviour. This task is certainly daunting and may in fact be impossible to achieve to the satisfaction of all concerned. The management of sex offenders, like all other client groups within the field of social work or criminal justice, reflects the political mood of the day, the stage of social change and the emerging theoretical and research developments.

PBNI, like all other statutory and voluntary agencies, contributes as well as responds to the direction of social change in our society. Best practice at an advanced level is therefore an ever-evolving process that takes account of, and responds to, such developments. Garland (1997, p 138) describes the work of probation as having:

> shifted from reforming offenders to managing risk and delivering expressive punishments; from a preventative role to a public protection role; and from rehabilitation centred on the person to rehabilitation as an instrument of control and risk management.

Changes in child protection thinking and the development of skills and experience of working with sex offenders have resulted in PBNI's recognition as an integral partner in the child and adult protection systems in our society. The Alderwood Centre was set up by PBNI in 1990 to develop specialist knowledge and provide multi-disciplinary treatment programmes for sex offenders. Practice experience at the Alderwood Centre, alongside legislative changes, highlighted the need for offenders to be managed in a dynamic and integrated way. Thus, in November 1997, the Integrated Supervision Unit (ISU) was established. An operational manager and a programme development manager head the ISU, based at the Alderwood Centre, with some staff located throughout the greater Belfast area. The team consists of social work staff from probation, social services and NSPCC, with other disciplines such as psychology and psychiatry playing key roles. Work undertaken by the unit contributes to an integrated system of managing and supervising sex offenders in the community and requires close working relationships with police, social services, hostels, housing and other agencies. The system works best when the offender, his family and significant others in his life are actively engaged in the process.

Gaps in practice

Whilst detailed manuals of guidance normally exist in respect of treatment programmes for sex offenders, practice experience suggested that the process of supervision was often found to be a mixture of implementing procedures and picking up on individual interests or styles of working. Addressing lifestyle issues was often reactionary, uncoordinated and *ad hoc*. Home visits were infrequent because the purpose of intervention was not clear. Attendance on an offending behaviour programme offered the naïve reassurance that this fulfilled the contact requirement.

In June 1997 a working party, set up to examine practice and identify gaps in the work with sex offenders, put forward the following findings for consideration by PBNI:

- a lack of consistency of approach to the supervision of sex offenders in respect of assessment, recording of information, profiling of lifestyle and the demands of the supervision process
- gaps in service provision, particularly in relation to access to treatment
- a need for strategic direction from PBNI
- a need for staff training in areas related to both supervision and treatment
- gaps in the community's awareness of the role of the PBNI in relation to sex offenders
- a need for child protection procedures to be updated in light of the new Children Order (NI) 1995
- a need for accommodation for sex offenders in the community.

As part of a series of responses to address these gaps and needs, a group of experienced staff was tasked with the responsibility of developing a practice guidance manual for the supervision of sex offenders in the community.

The approach to developing the manual of guidance

Adhering to the principle of learning from others' experience, one of the tasks undertaken on behalf of the sex offender working party was to examine practice guidelines for the supervision of sex offenders by other probation services in England and Wales. Whilst a range of documents existed, some relating to policy, some to practice issues, it was difficult to find a practice manual or indeed any document that comprehensively addressed the issue of supervision of sex offenders from both a strategic and practice perspective.

A survey by the Association of Chief Probation Officers (ACPO) in 1996, *Community Based Interventions with Sex Offenders Organised by Probation Services* (Proctor and Flaxington), revealed significant progress in service provision over the previous five to six years, particularly in respect of the development of treatment programmes. PBNI's Alderwood Centre was among those projects identified as having a higher number of programmes and a broader range of interventions, thus accommodating a larger number of clients. It was clear from the survey that probation services throughout Britain had made significant developments and improvements in relation to work with sex offenders in the early 1990s. By the mid-1990s, 82 per cent of probation services had issued specific sex offender policy statements. Over half the services had produced a strategy for supervising sex offenders and 88 per cent were delivering specialist programmes.

As part of the process I searched the Internet for material on the supervision of sex offenders in the US. Much of the material for treatment programmes in Britain has been developed from work carried out there. However, the US probation services are somewhat different in structure and most treatment programmes are developed, not by probation, but by psychology services; probation usually assumes the role of law enforcement with offenders, in contrast to the vision of PBNI where the proposal has been to integrate the two aspects of intervention. It is, however, worth observing the direction and focus PBNI may take in the coming years, given the move towards law enforcement by probation services in England and Wales. It is vital that the need for behavioural change is not lost in the battle for public protection.

Because of its size, the US has a range of experiences to learn from. In many states there is evidence of quite sophisticated systems for co-operation across disciplines. In Massachusetts, for example, parole officers work as part of a team with sex offender counsellors and a state police polygrapher to supervise sex offenders in the community. The programme uses electronic monitoring, polygraph testing, surveillance, frequent unannounced home visits, work and community visits, drug testing, curfews and individual sex offender counselling (Hubbard, 1996). In contrast, Washington DC has no state-funded sex offender programmes: the courts impose lengthy custodial sentences for all types of sex crime. The state is now funding research into examining the effectiveness of other means of dealing with such crime.

Northern Ireland, as a relatively small country with only one police force, one probation service, and four health boards, has the opportunity to learn from the experience of others and to work in an integrated way. Each agency has a responsibility to give its staff guidance that meets its needs and takes account of inter-disciplinary protocols. The need also for a province-wide, interdisciplinary and strategic approach has long been called for, and is currently being developed.

The PBNI management of sex offenders manual: a guide to practice

This manual has put in place guidance and procedures for managing and supervising sex offenders. A separate programme manual describes offending behaviour programmes available within PBNI. The Board's mission statement in respect of their work with sex offenders outlines the basis for intervention:

> PBNI, where appropriate, in collaboration with other agencies and with the community, will provide programmes of supervision and support which help prevent re-offending in sex offenders and in doing so contribute to public protection (PBNI 1998, p 2).

The manual is a comprehensive, working document. In its corporate plan PBNI committed itself to the principle that all practice will be research-led and grounded within a sound theoretical framework. The literature and research sections thus provide a range of material from a national and international perspective that provides the reader with a sound knowledge base, hopefully sparking a desire to explore particular areas of interest. This section also provides the worker with an understanding of the context in which agency practice is grounded.

Working in a small region such as Northern Ireland often means that professionals have to rely on research and statistical information from other countries where cultures and social norms differ. This is true for work with sexual abuse. It is only in recent years that British and Irish writers have begun to produce material: the work of Morrison, Erooga and Beckett (1994) and Travers (1999) is of note. Statistical information on sex offenders within Northern Ireland is outlined, with particular reference to the Northern Ireland Incidence Study in 1991. This is the only province-wide research on the incidence of sexual abuse in Northern Ireland. Recent studies such as Leonard's (2000) will be included in the annual process of review and updating. The section on operational guidelines includes both procedural matters and recommendations for good practice. The Abuse of Trust Inquiry in Northern Ireland (1993, p 125) advised:

> Organisations or individuals receiving concerns about the activities or planned activities of sex offenders should ensure that full details of the concerns are elicited, recorded and communicated accurately. Information should be verified; subsequent decisions based on established fact, rather on conjecture.

Effective communication between relevant professionals is essential. In order for this to occur, procedures and protocols must be in place. Thus, the manual lays out procedures for the fast and efficient sharing of information on a regular basis between those workers involved in the process of supervision. The supervising probation officer is therefore advised of the need to visit the offender at his home on a regular basis, but at varied times, announced and unannounced, in the evenings or afternoons, as well as Saturday mornings. A picture of the offender's lifestyle can then emerge: what is in his house, who calls, how he is perceived in the neighbourhood, where he goes, what he does and with whom. Information is gained not only through home visits but also through regular contact with specialist probation programmes, local police, social services, and other community providers as required. The composite picture needs to be shared, and strategies agreed and reviewed in regular multi-disciplinary meetings.

This integrated approach reduces differences between regions and between agencies. In order to learn from previous tragedies it is important to build in a system of monitoring and communicating. Procedures that are not followed or do not work effectively in practice must be identified and addressed. In 1995, Morrison examined effective communication between organisations and concluded that partnership is a crucial concept that agencies must get right, and this meant building trust. Systems, such as those outlined in the manual, that allow for and demand a high level of inter-agency co-operation and communication go some way to engendering understanding and trust. Joint working leads to the development of professional relationships, relationships create understanding, and understanding nurtures co-operation and collaboration. Collaboration and trust allow for shared responsibility and decision-making.

Working with sex offenders calls upon personal resources and feelings that may not reveal themselves in other areas of work. In this context, Erooga (1994, p 210) advises:

> Professional values do not exist independently of wider social forces and

> interests. As well as a need to be clear about the causes of, and offenders' responsibility for, sexual abuse, it is also important for workers to be aware of these wider influences and their own values and beliefs about sexuality, which will influence not only their practice, but also the personal impact of the work.

It is vital therefore that organisations recognise some of the dilemmas and challenges of the work and set a baseline against which practitioners can measure success. The principles and values reflected in the manual attempt to set a context in which individuals are encouraged to explore their own personal values and beliefs. It reflects and incorporates PBNI's general principles and values for working with all offenders and includes specific points about sex offending, taking into account Salter (1988), Morrison (1994), the work of The Association for the Treatment of Sexual Abusers (1997) in the US and the National Organisation for Treatment of Abusers (NOTA), a British equivalent.

A significant factor in relation to the value base for working with sex offenders is the issue of balancing the rights and needs of victims with the rights of the offender to lead his life free from oppression. For staff to feel comfortable and confident with a supervision process that includes a level of surveillance, it is vital that they are clear about the principles and values that underlie their practice. Working with a group so controversial and personally challenging as sex offenders forces one to consider the inner costs. This in turn grounds practice in a principle-centred approach.

The way forward

The process of putting the guidance into practice has highlighted the gaps where stronger relationships need to be forged. Currently, the most difficult area of practice for the effective management of sex offenders in the community is finding and sustaining appropriate accommodation. As the agency responsible for housing in the public sector the Northern Ireland Housing Executive (NIHE) has become a new and increasingly important partner in this field of work. Whilst relationships are being forged at practice level it is of the utmost importance that such collaboration is translated into the development of protocols between all relevant bodies to address the issue of accommodation. Development in practice and provision of accommodation for sex offenders must take account of a range of needs. A relatively small number of sex offenders need long-term, secure and supervised accommodation. Others require hostel-style accommodation for a specified period where issues of resettlement can be addressed. Others will require independent accommodation within communities where the rights of children and the general public must be balanced against the rights of the individual offender.

There is a great need for partnership with the community if we are to work towards a truly effective means of managing this type of offender. Much work is needed by all of the agencies together to bring about community education, support, guidance and recognition. However, before opening the debate fully to the public and preparing for mainstream community education, those with statutory responsibility, knowledge and expertise must first come together under a common strategy. In responding to the original question of whether we are able to provide an effective response to the management of sex offenders in our community, it is important to view the changes and developments in practice in the context of government strategic planning in Northern Ireland. The key agencies tasked with the responsibility of managing this group of offenders have moved forward within a model of collaboration and co-operation. The experience of the probation officer supervising a sex offender is of working closely with staff on specialist programmes of intervention (those staff may include a child protection social worker), with Social Services in the community, visiting hostels and working with hostel staff, working with NIHE staff and police CARE unit staff. This model of working must be rooted in sound policy and guidance that ensures close collaboration in times of tension and conflict.

In response to a ground-swell of opinion from agencies working together in the field of child protection and criminal justice, the Northern Ireland Office (NIO) has brought together a comprehensive range of departments and agencies to produce an agreed province-wide strategy for the management of sex offenders. This strategic plan has passed consultation stage and its launch is pending. The 'Northern Ireland Manual of Inter-Agency Guidance' consultation document (1999) outlines the need for guidance and proposes a model for risk assessment and risk management of sex offenders in the community. Its purpose is to 'meet the requirements of current legislation, build good practice and protect the public' (NIO, p 4).

The response to this document has generally been positive. All disciplines working within the field of sexual abuse and child protection welcome strategic planning and guidance on an inter-disciplinary basis; it recognises and acknowledges the complex and demanding nature of this work. The document reflects the fact that good practice is happening, but if it is to be sustained and developed it requires strategic support and guidance from agencies. The consultation process has created the opportunity for debate between agencies and for dynamic thinking. The response to the document has urged the need for refinement of the proposed procedures to reflect the already known demands of practice. Those who know best what kind of guidance they require are not to be found in the higher echelons of government; they are at the front line of practice. The document has not yet reached main grade practitioners, those who will ultimately have the responsibility to carry out the policy and procedures. The delay in producing and implementing the guidance may be due to the uncertain political and social future of Northern Ireland. It is vital that, whatever that future may hold, the prospects for real social development should not be lost or delayed.

Conclusion

Change and development have now become an ongoing and integral part of life as we begin a new millennium. In reaching that historical date, the pace of such change has increased, some would say to the point where we are at risk of spinning out of control. One wonders if such a pace can be maintained throughout this millennium and beyond or will we reach a peak, a lull, a time for reflection. Kolb's (1991) cycle of learning suggests that we will. In taking up the challenge to undertake and implement major change and practice development it is of vital importance that agencies and organisations watch their cycle of learning carefully and take time for reflection and evaluation. It is of equal importance that in doing so the agency maintains the impetus to seek further development as an outcome of that reflection.

If sex offenders are a part of our communities, whether we like it or not the demand for effective methods of supervision has become a significant driving force for change. PBNI have faced this demand and recognise the need for partnership with other bodies to meet it. The development of the manual of guidance for specialist staff has been one step in the process. The development of integrated provision of supervision and treatment on an inter-agency basis gives us the means to move forward in partnership. Developing true partnership involves not only having procedures and protocols; it is just as important to develop relationships at all levels. The guidance outlined in the practice manual has created the opportunity for professional relationships to be developed at both intra- and interagency levels. It remains to be seen if the same strategic developments can be achieved at departmental and government levels.

References

Association for the Treatment of Sexual Abusers (1997) *Ethical Standards and Principles for the Management of Sexual Abusers*, Oregon: ATSA

Becker, J. and Kaplin, M. (1988) *The Assessment of Adolescent Sex Offenders*, New York: Sage Publications

Erooga, M. (1994) 'Where the Professional meets the Personal', in Morrison, T., Erooga, M. and Beckett, R. (eds.) *Sexual Offending Against Children*, London: Routledge

Garland, D. (1993) *Probation and the Reconfiguration of Crime Control*, London: Goddard & Hiller

Hubbard, S. (1996) *Intensive Parole For Sex Offenders*, USA: Massachusetts State Parole Board

Kolb, D. (1991) *Organisational Behaviour, An Experimental Approach*, New Jersey: Prentice Hall

Morrison, T. (1994) 'Context, Constraints and Considerations for Practice', in Morrison, T. Erooga, M. and Beckett, R. (eds.) *Sexual Offending Against Children*. London: Routledge

Northern Ireland Office (1999) *Procedures for the Assessment and Management of Risk of Sex Offenders and Offenders against Children: Northern Ireland Manual of Inter-Agency Guidance*, Belfast: NIO

Probation Board for Northern Ireland (1998) *Manual of Guidance on Supervision of Sex Offenders*, Belfast: PBNI

Proctor, E. and Flaxington, F. (1996) *Community Based Interventions with Sex Offenders Organised by Probation Services: A Survey Of Current Practice*, UK: Association of Chief Probation Officers

Roberts, C. (1991) 'What Works: Using Social Work Methods to Reduce Reoffending in Serious and Persistent Offenders', *Applied Social Studies*, University of Oxford

Salter, A. (1988) *Treating Child Sex Offenders and their Victims – A Practical Guide*. Beverly Hills, CA: Sage Publications

Social Services Inspectorate (1993) *An Abuse of Trust Enquiry*, Belfast: HMSO

Tomison, A. (1995) 'Update On Child Sexual Abuse'. Nation Child Protection Clearing House Issues, Paper No. 5, Australia: Australian Institute of Family Studies

Travers, O. (1999) *Behind the Silhouettes: Exploring the Myths of Sexual Abuse*, Dublin: Blackstaff

7 Staff are citizens too! Promoting practice development within agencies

Christine Smyth

Introduction

Health and Personal Social Services (HPSS) in Northern Ireland has operated and will continue to operate in a situation of continuing organisational change and political uncertainty for the forceseeable future. The 1990s saw unprecedented change in the organisation, management and delivery of health and personal social services. The twenty-first century heralds yet more changes with proposals to introduce primary care arrangements for the delivery of health and social care, major changes in the organisation of personal social services education and training and the planned introduction of a General Social Care Council, illustrating the continuing complexity and breadth of the change agenda ahead. As these nationally and locally agreed initiatives come on stream they will create yet more challenges requiring people to adapt, change and develop how they work in order to accommodate the new arrangements and meet the new requirements.

Review of the literature

The ongoing need for organisations to balance increasing demands and higher expectations with the same or even fewer resources, while at the same time retaining the support and commitment of their staff, poses a major challenge. The managerialism introduced into the public sector in the 1990s with its emphasis on effectiveness, efficiency and economy does not appear to have achieved this balance. Studies into the impact of organisational change on staff in the 1990s found that morale, self-esteem and performance had been adversely affected (Carnall, 1990; Holbeche, 1997). One Northern Ireland consultancy company warned that organisations were 'dangerously blind to the damage done by the destruction of employee loyalty as a result of new working practices' (Kirk, 1997).

Continuing legislative and policy changes such as the Children Order (NI) 1995 and *People First* (1990) have challenged both agencies and practitioners to work differently. There has been a significant shift from a generic model of social work provision to an increasingly specialist model. At the same time, practitioners have had to take on new roles, develop alternative approaches and demonstrate the principles of partnership and empowerment in practice.

These developments imply changes in the ways social workers practise and the skills and qualities required of them. Practice development is therefore as crucial as organisational development to implementing the requirements of new legislation and policies. But how far do organisations create the conditions that encourage and support practitioners to experiment and innovate, to be flexible and responsive? According to Pottage and Evans (1996) the evolution of the practice knowledge base is not keeping pace with organisational change and the workplace is primarily 'a field of operations' and not 'a field of learning'.

Pottage and Evans state that meaningful innovation and development must emanate from informed and intelligent operational staff. This reservoir of expertise remains largely untapped in most organisations, a view echoed by modern management theorists and writers. Senge (1990), Covey (1992), Handy (1994), and Simmons (1996) have long urged organisations to create and harness more positive working environments with an emphasis on people and values rather than on roles and efficiency-obsessed activities. Listening to the experience of operational staff about how services and practice need to evolve is an essential precondition if innovative and user-centred practice is to flourish (Pottage and Evans).

Senge (p 4) wrote that 'the organisations that will truly excel in the future will be the organisations that discover how to tap people's commitment and capacity to learn at all levels'. Learning has to be greater or at least equal to the degree of change; this requires conditions where behaviours and practices of continuous development are actively encouraged (Mayo and Lank, 1995; Mumford, 1995). This is, in essence, the concept of the 'learning organisation', or what Pottage and Evans refer to as the competent workplace, one which facilitates the learning of all its members and continually transforms itself.

Context of study

Senior managers within a Community Trust were aware that the continual pressure of major organisational changes over the years had made considerable demands on staff in terms of increased workloads, loyalty and goodwill. There was a recognition of the need to invest in staff and to support them to meet the ongoing demands for change and improvement. Middle and first-line managers were identified as key players in helping achieve the Trust's stated objective of providing a supportive and challenging environment for all staff as they played a key role in leading and managing the change agenda within the Trust.

Through an exploration of managers' own experiences it was hoped to identify the organisational and management conditions that help and facilitate staff to deliver quality services against a backdrop of continuous change. This was the context for a survey of 35 managers from different professional backgrounds with the objective of examining the factors that either blocked or facilitated learning and support of staff. Its results would inform the design of development initiatives, building on existing good practices and moving the Trust towards its objective of becoming 'a learning organisation'.

The Trust had taken on significant aspects of the general management ethos with a commitment to break down professional barriers and promote multi-disciplinary team-working and cross-skilling; the sample of managers chosen to participate in the study reflected this professional mix. It was agreed with the senior management team that managers from the largest operational division in the Trust (Adult Services) and one support division (Human Resources) would participate. Factors influencing the selection of the divisions included:

- the perceived pressures within divisions and capacity of staff to participate
- the perceived representation of health and social care interests at operational level
- senior managers' commitment to support the survey and subsequent work derived from it.

Figure 7.1 Profile of middle managers

Background	Number	Responsibility
Social work (6)	4	Unidisciplinary social work service
	2	Multidisciplinary service
Nursing (4)	2	Unidisciplinary nurse service
	2	Multidisciplinary service
Allied to medicine	1	Unidisciplinary service (podiatry)
Human resources	2	

Note: Job titles of middle managers do not relate to traditional professional jobs in line with the general management ethos. Middle managers with a social work background equate with either Asst Principal Social Worker or Principal Social Worker grades, reflecting the merger of these two management levels within a flatter hierarchical structure

Middle managers

Thirteen middle managers were interviewed, eight from Adult Services and five from Human Resources (see Figure 7.1). The managers were selected by their heads of department to ensure representation of different areas within divisions. The head of Adult Services also wanted to ensure that managers overloaded by new work initiatives would not be put under additional pressure.

All managers worked full-time and were white Europeans. Five were male and eight female. Six were from a Protestant background, seven from a Catholic background. The following user groups were represented: mental health, learning disability, elderly, physical health and disability, and sensory impairment. Community, residential, day care and hospital settings were also represented, as were specialist support areas including education and training, and occupational health.

Figure 7.2 Profile of first-line managers

Background	Number	Responsibility
Social work (SSW) (11)	5	Unidisciplinary team
	3	Multidisciplinary (learning disability, mental health, elder care)
	3	No direct staff management responsibility
Human resources (5)	3	Direct staff management responsibility
	2	No direct staff management responsibility
Allied to medicine (3)	2	Unidisciplinary team (speech therapy, podiatry)
	1	No direct staff management responsibility
Nursing (2)	1	Unidisciplinary team
	1	No direct staff management responsibility
Administration	1	Multidisciplinary

Note: Professional job titles were more in evidence among first-line managers, as were traditional professional management structures

First-line managers

Twenty-two managers were identified in total, fourteen from Adult Services and eight from Human Resources (see Figure 7.2). Nineteen were employed at first-line management grade or equivalent. The three remaining staff were employed on administrative grades but reported directly to middle managers in Human Resources.

Twenty managers worked full time with two in a job share arrangement. All were white Europeans, fifteen from a Protestant and seven from a Catholic background. Seven managers were male and fifteen female.

Methodology

Semi-structured interviews were used to gather qualitative data about the opinions, views and subjective experiences of managers. A thematic approach was adopted which allowed issues to be mapped, such as changes and their impact on roles and responsibilities, challenges and opportunities presented by the changes and the factors that had either supported staff, or not, to meet these challenges and opportunities. This approach involved a critical review of existing support systems and the identification of what needed to change to create the conditions that would allow staff to give their best.

What essentially was a listening exercise achieved three things. First, it began the process of involving and engaging managers and creating an awareness of the need for change, thereby setting the stage for subsequent action. Secondly, recommendations for any changes to organisational or management practices recognised existing good practices and addressed issues identified by the managers themselves. Thirdly and perhaps most importantly, the process of thinking about their own experiences was valued by participants and proved to be an impetus for some to be proactive in beginning to address their own particular problems. It seemed that the process of reflecting on their situation acted as a catalyst for action to improve existing practices.

These outcomes outweighed the difficulties of using semi-structured interviews as a means of gathering information, including the time involved and the difficulties in analysing and interpreting the data. Just as in social work, the process itself was as important as the outcome. All the quotations on the following pages were recorded at these interviews.

Outcomes

The study highlighted the significant impact of flatter management structures on the volume, diversity and span of responsibilities of managers. Loyalty to the organisation, motivation, job satisfaction and attitudes to organisational and practice changes appeared to be affected by how people had been managed and supported through the changes. Three key elements emerged that are of particular relevance to the identification of factors that support and facilitate staff continuously to develop practice and service delivery:

- ***Direction and purpose:*** clarity regarding what is expected of them and the degree of autonomy they have to carry it out
- ***Guidance and support:*** planned, individual time with line manager; help with problem-solving; guided not directed; supported, especially when things go wrong; pressure of work recognised; acknowledgement
- ***Learning and development:*** feedback; opportunities to learn on the job; balance of focus on results, processes and inputs; development planning

Direction and purpose

Respondents with a clear understanding of their brief, with 'real' devolved responsibility and authority, viewed their jobs and the changes more positively. Almost half of the first-line managers and one quarter of the middle managers reported lack of clarity regarding expectations and reporting lines. They also believed they had received contradictory messages regarding the parameters of their authority: on the one hand they were told they had the authority for work; on the other they were told what to do:

> I am happy with the delegation of responsibility as long as I know what I'm responsible for – how much authority do I really have?

All managers wanted senior management to take an interest in their work. Most of the first line managers thought that senior management did not understand their work or the pressures they were under:

> I feel that senior managers don't know what we do on an average day. They should keep in touch with reality.

Positive views were expressed about senior managers who visited workplaces and listened to staff concerns. Even if changes did not result, staff felt that at least they had had the opportunity to put their viewpoint forward.

Guidance and support

An extensive range of support systems existed and line managers, peers and networks were identified as the top three supports. All respondents except two viewed their line managers as their main source of support and wanted formal, planned, one-to-one meetings with them. Only 57% (20) of the total sample reported that this happened routinely; they were generally more satisfied with their support than managers who did not have any dedicated time with their line manager:

> If you want to get the best out of people and push them to their maximum you need to support them.

The ability of line managers to listen to the views of their staff, take their concerns seriously and welcome and value ideas was seen to be an important attribute of effective support:

> My line manager is willing to listen and values my opinion – it's more like a partnership.

Several managers expressed the view that line managers who only heard what they wanted to hear and who could not deal with criticism and challenge blocked staff initiative and enthusiasm.

All managers expressed a strong commitment to supporting their own staff but many felt increased workloads and responsibilities had eroded the time available to do so. The two most quoted activities for supporting staff were team meetings and operating an 'open door' policy. Staff managed by an 'open door' policy only did not think this system was satisfactory as individuals had to ask for time, which was difficult when managers were seen to be busy. There was also concern that using the system could be interpreted as a 'sign of weakness or an indication you couldn't cope'.

All first-line managers with a social work background who were responsible for managing staff provided formal supervision to their staff. Over half of these managers thought that 'supervision has been weakened dramatically'. This was blamed on the flatter management structures and increased workloads. While support and development of staff were thought to be important components of supervision, these elements tended to be subservient to the accountability agenda:

> Supervision deals purely with case management issues – the focus is on accountability. The focus on development needs has suffered.

The fact that supervision had become largely prescriptive and systematised, with an emphasis on compliance and procedures, meant it did not fulfil its potential as a vehicle to support learning and development.

Middle managers with a social work background suggested that the blanket application (i.e. once a month) of supervision to all social workers, especially experienced ones:

> encouraged defensive practice and did not develop the confidence and capacity of social workers to act relatively independently within their own level of competence.

They were also critical that supervision did not focus sufficiently on the outcomes or effectiveness of social work interventions. Although critical of current supervisory systems, the general view of managers was that all staff should receive some form of support from their manager.

While first-line managers of social workers overwhelmingly expressed concern about keeping abreast of practice developments and managing experienced staff, middle managers expressed the view that managers did not have to be experts in the area of practice in order to manage effectively or help their staff develop. Rather, they needed to develop their own competence and to have confidence in the ability of their staff to make decisions and do the work.

Over three-quarters of respondents valued peers as a major source of support and learning. This support was informal and opportunistic. Time, volume of work and accessibility were three of the main factors affecting opportunities to link with peers:

> It can feel quite isolated working on your own with little cross-fertilisation ... people are so busy you don't want to intrude.

Positive views were expressed about the mutual support derived from meeting as a staff team. The level of support from this forum appeared to be influenced by the style of leadership and whether it was perceived as facilitating co-operative working relationships or controlling in nature.

Networks were valued as supports by almost half the sample. Objectivity and a different perspective were the two main benefits derived. External networks, particularly with staff from other Trusts, were thought to have been diminished by the organisational changes. This was seen to be a loss. Staff in specialist posts (e.g. speech therapy) were more likely to maintain external networks for professional support. Only one fifth of the sample (7) stated they used professional associations to keep up-to-date with professional issues and developments. These staff were from nursing or a profession allied to medicine.

Learning and development

The fact that the roles and responsibilities of both managers and practitioners are continuously evolving means that staff are having to acquire new knowledge, develop new skills and learn to do things differently:

> There's a need to change the way you think about things and do things – that takes a certain amount of time and personal pain.

Eight of the sixteen staff who had taken on entirely new roles in the survey felt supported and helped 'to learn the ropes'; the others felt 'disheartened by the lack of support'.

While formal training was quoted as a way of developing the new knowledge and skills required, it was also thought to have limitations, particularly in terms of timeliness, relevance and practical application. Learning on the job was thought to be important although this tended to be unstructured, unplanned and retrospective. Collaborative working, observing others, feedback and reflection were identified as useful ways of learning on the job, but pressure on staff time meant that these activities were seen as a luxury and not actively encouraged:

> The current climate compels acting rather than thinking.

Everyone had received informal coaching on the job. This was primarily reactive and problem-specific, focusing on putting in the skills and knowledge required to achieve a particular task. The emphasis on tasks and results meant that less effort was put into improving and helping staff performance. Some people expressed the view that there needed to be a balance between the one-off, reactive, problem-solving approach and a planned, proactive, developmental approach.

All staff wanted formal and explicit feedback about their work which they believed would make them feel valued and appreciated and would also encourage them to improve and develop further:

> Staff need to be told how they are doing, it helps their confidence.

> There's a lack of appreciation; if things are going well it's taken for granted.

> I would like some feedback and affirmation – some way of measuring how well I'm doing.

No one claimed to know on a consistent basis how well they were doing in their work:

> I judge how well I'm doing by the least number of disasters.

All middle managers were involved in annual staff appraisal. There was general support for the concept:

> The discipline of being able to show what you've done and credit for how you fit into the bigger picture is an opportunity to get more job satisfaction.

One formal meeting a year to review progress was thought to be inadequate. Annual performance objectives concentrated mainly on expected work outcomes and rarely on development needs. There was no mechanism to ensure the appraisal system cascaded through the organisation to staff at all levels, resulting in inconsistency in application throughout the Trust.

Implications for managing and developing practice

The implications of the findings from this study are now considered in the context of supporting and facilitating the continuous development of social work practice. From the findings it is possible to identify factors which impact on staff morale, motivation and sense of job satisfaction (see Figure 7.3). The factors that contribute to improving morale, motivation and satisfaction also support learning and development.

Figure 7.3 Factors impacting on staff morale, motivation and job satisfaction

Factors IMPROVING morale, motivation and satisfaction	Factors REDUCING morale, motivation and satisfaction
Clear expectations	Uncertainty or mixed messages
Clear parameters for authority and accountability	Lack of authority and accountability
New and challenging opportunities	Overload or underload
Ongoing feedback	No feedback
Empowerment	Control
Recognition/feedback	Lack of recognition
Relationships	Isolation
Two-way communication	Top-down communication only
Practivity, forward planning	Reactivity
Process and outcome focus	Outcome focus only

Note: Professional job titles were more in evidence among first-line managers, as were traditional professional management structures

From control to empowerment

The survey findings suggest that staff who are empowered by their managers are generally more highly motivated to take on new challenges and develop their practice in light of changing circumstances. What does empowering staff involve? In looking at the survey and what the literature tells us (Covey, 1996; Smale, 1996) there is a consensus about the following key elements:

- clear expectations of what is required
- clearly defined parameters
- delegated responsibility and personal accountability
- information and resources necessary to accomplish the task

- a sense of partnership with one's manager based on mutual respect and trust.

Traditional organisational cultures and management styles based on command and control (which are procedurally driven) will not foster empowerment. Instructing staff simply to follow procedures in a subservient manner may make them dependent on others, stifling creativity and independent, critical thinking.

It would of course be irresponsible to suggest that procedural frameworks should be ignored, but research confirms that procedures are too readily called into play at the expense of ethical informed practice (DOH, 1995; Kearney, 1996). Ideally, procedures should support and guide workers and provide a safety net above which creative, useful and ethically informed practice can be developed.

Improvements and developments in practice will only be achieved by focusing on people, relationships and processes as well as outcomes and balance sheets. To achieve this, it is not enough for senior managers to demand that others do things differently. Senior managers themselves have to change how they approach their work and relate to others within the organisation. This involves changing not just behaviours and ways of working but more fundamentally changing the belief systems and thinking that underpin and perpetuate current management behaviours: 'The challenge is to be a light, not a judge; to be a model, not a critic' (Covey, p 25).

If organisations can succeed in empowering their staff it is more likely that staff will succeed in empowering clients and their carers as they practise in an environment that recognises and values the experiences and dilemmas of those involved in delivering and receiving the service.

From management to leadership

The survey overwhelmingly confirms the crucial role and impact of managers and management styles on staff morale, motivation and job satisfaction. The following behaviours were identified as positive enablers for staff:

- treating staff with respect
- demonstrating personal integrity
- having high expectations of staff
- focusing on people-development
- giving regular and ongoing feedback on staff performance
- providing trust, encouragement and support to staff
- an openness to ideas from staff
- welcome staff's challenge to the *status quo*
- actively managing change, especially the people aspect
- dealing constructively with conflicts.

These behaviours suggest a shift away from the management paradigm where people are 'managed' with the expectation that they are paid to do what they are told, towards a new paradigm of leadership where the manager becomes a leader of leaders rather than a leader of followers (Simmons, 1996). Lao-Tzu (paraphrased in Senge, 1990, p 41) wisely counsels:

> The bad leader is he who the people despise. The good leader is he who the people praise. The great leader is he of whom the people say: we did it ourselves.

The expectation that managers can manage in ways that are different to how they were or are managed ignores the fact that they too need assistance to develop new ways of working. Developing management capacity needs to be a priority so that appropriate leadership styles can be developed that empower individuals and teams.

From training to continuous improvement

The need for practice continuously to evolve and develop to keep pace with changes means there is a need for constant staff development. Ironically, as the demand and need for learning and development have increased, the time and resources available to commit to it have reduced.

A major but underutilised source of learning comes from doing the job. Learning from experience is not a well-developed skill and is rarely formally encouraged (Pearn *et al.*, 1995). Given that it is largely an unstructured and unplanned activity one could surmise that much of the potential for learning is actually lost as individuals do not reflect on or draw conclusions from their experience (Kolb, 1983).

If managers are to be expected to use structured on-the-job opportunities to develop practitioners' capacity to learn from their practice and to develop continuously they will again have to think about the skills and competence required to achieve this. One does not have to look far for a development programme that focuses on developing competence in facilitating and managing learning: the Practice Teacher's Award Programme.

While managers are clearly central to encouraging and supporting learning and development, their availability and accessibility have been affected by increased workloads and flatter management structures. The potential of peers and networks to contribute to learning and support does not appear to have been fully realised or exploited within organisations. In fact, organisational structures and rising workloads were thought to have diminished learning opportunities in terms of peer contact and networks. Managers wishing to encourage new forms of practice need to foster peer and network relationships and allocate time for staff to explore and examine new ideas with others.

From supervision to practice development

Theoretically, social work supervision provides the framework and opportunity to manage, support and develop the practice of social workers, yet this potential has not been realised. Managers themselves are dissatisfied with the form and content of supervision; studies also indicate that experienced workers tend to be even more dissatisfied with supervision because they do not find it sufficiently challenging or developmental (Payne, 1994). The intelligence and first-hand knowledge of staff at the front line should be used in planning and decision-making for practice and service developments and in problem-solving, but this does not appear to be happening.

Implicit in the word 'supervision' are meanings such as inspection, direction, and overseeing. The current practice of supervision seems to support these definitions. The term does not encapsulate the supportive and developmental aspects which all parties to the supervision process claim to value.

Finding new ways to express old ideas, while not of themselves enough to achieve change, can at least highlight and make explicit the desired change in attitude and behaviour. The renaming of supervision would also address the current realities for some social workers who access professional guidance outside the traditional line management/supervisory structures.

While the role of the first line manager must continue to include accountability for staff, practice and service delivery, the terminology for planned one-to-one meetings could become something more focused on practice and development. 'Practice consultation', 'practice development clinic', 'progress report' and 'practice update' are possible alternatives that emphasise the practice component and the sense of shared responsibility and development.

The survey findings, along with the author's knowledge and experience of

- supervising and assessing practice against competence requirements
- occupational standards and their application in staff appraisal and supervision systems
- developing a quality assurance systems for social work practice based on a standards and audit approach (Smyth *et al.*, 1999)
- developing a performance management approach based on coaching and mentoring models

reinforce the importance of focusing not just on expected results and outcomes but on the inputs and processes to achieve the results if development of, and learning from, practice are to be encouraged and supported.

A model for practice development comprising these three elements – outcomes, processes and inputs – reinforces the developmental role of the manager and focuses learning on and through work (see Figure 7.4). This ensures that the three key requirements of support – direction and purpose, guidance and support, and development – are met.

Figure 7.4 A practice development model

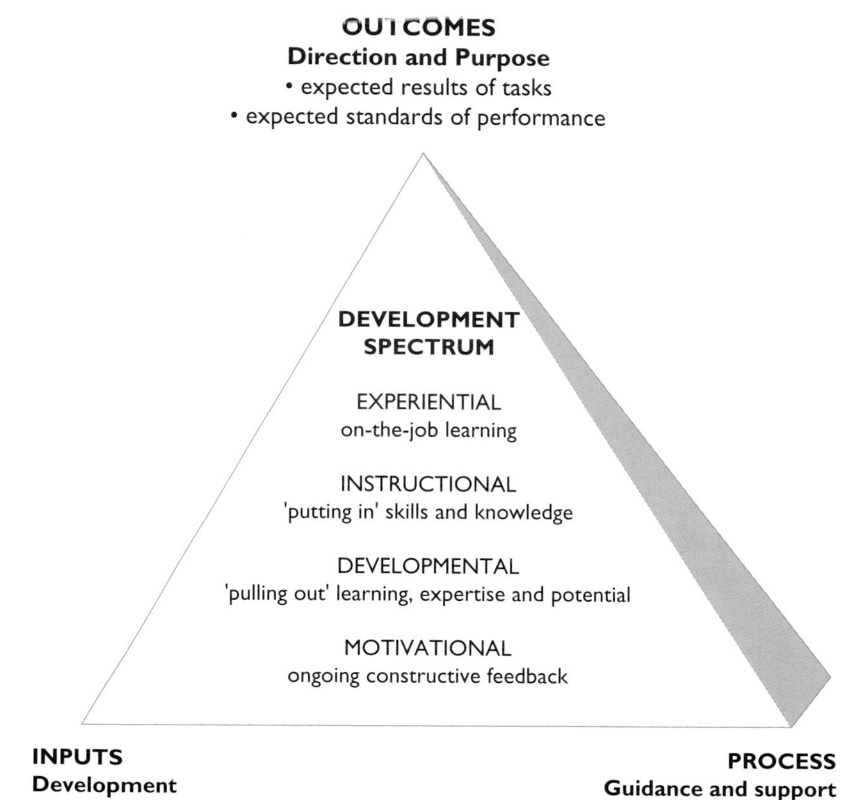

In consultation with the worker, the line manager begins by clarifying what the purpose of involvement is in particular pieces of work. This is developed further to identify what the worker hopes to achieve (outcomes) in their work with the individual, family, group or community. These outcomes can be both short-term, i.e. the expected results at the end of a session; and long-term, i.e. the expected results at the end of a period of planned intervention.

Having clearly established the purpose and expected outcomes of the work, expected standards need to be discussed. Some agencies have established standards for various aspects of work. Where standards do not exist the worker, service user(s) and line manager may agree specific standards relevant to the particular situation. Direction, purpose and clear expectations are now established.

The next two steps in the process focus on guidance, support and development. While the manager needs to confirm that the worker is clear about the agreed protocols and procedures, this forms only part of the discussion about the process. The worker's thoughts on possible ways of intervening to achieve desired results need to be explored through a critical evaluation of the rationale for different interventions. This could be further expanded to meet the requirements of evidence-based practice with workers encouraged to base decisions about ways of working on evidence and research of what is effective in practice. The manager can monitor the range of interventions used by all workers within the team and encourage them to expand their repertoire, linking workers with each other to share different experiences and ways of working, thereby encouraging and facilitating peer support and professional development.

When the method of working (the process) has been negotiated and agreed with the service user, the resources, knowledge and skills required to deliver the planned intervention should be explored and monitored. Where there are gaps in the worker's knowledge or skill base it is the manager's responsibility to ensure that the worker is supported to gain the required competence to carry out the work.

At the heart of the practice development model is the development spectrum (see Figure 7.5), based on a coaching model. 'Coaching' is an ongoing process of assisting individuals and teams to improve their competence and performance by learning through work opportunities. The 'development spectrum' allows flexibility to meet the changing needs of the learner from newly qualified through to highly experienced and the changing requirements of the job. The line manager is responsible for providing opportunities that facilitate workers to develop their potential and expand their practice; this can either be instructional or developmental in nature. Instructional approaches involve teaching someone how to do something: 'putting in' either the knowledge or skills (developmental approaches involve helping people to realise their potential); and 'pulling out' learning and ideas.

The underlying philosophy of a coaching model (Kanter, 1989; Clutterbuck, 1992; Kalinauckas and King, 1994) is based on premises that:

- staff satisfaction and motivation are improved when ongoing feedback is given about performance and work
- staff practice is developed when new opportunities are identified to develop their capabilities with appropriate support and help
- staff are enabled to contribute to innovation and assume greater

responsibility and pride for their work when their efforts are appreciated and their achievements recognised.

Ongoing feedback is therefore a key element of the model. While line managers need to play the central role in facilitating, motivating and giving feedback to their staff, it is possible (and probably advisable) to identify and utilise the knowledge and expertise of other team members and colleagues as coaches for their peers. This would help dilute the expectation that a manager must be an expert in every aspect of practice, which is becoming more and more unrealistic with increasing specialisms and spans of responsibility. It also recognises the importance of peer support and other networks and begins to formalise and legitimise their activities.

Figure 7.5 The development spectrum

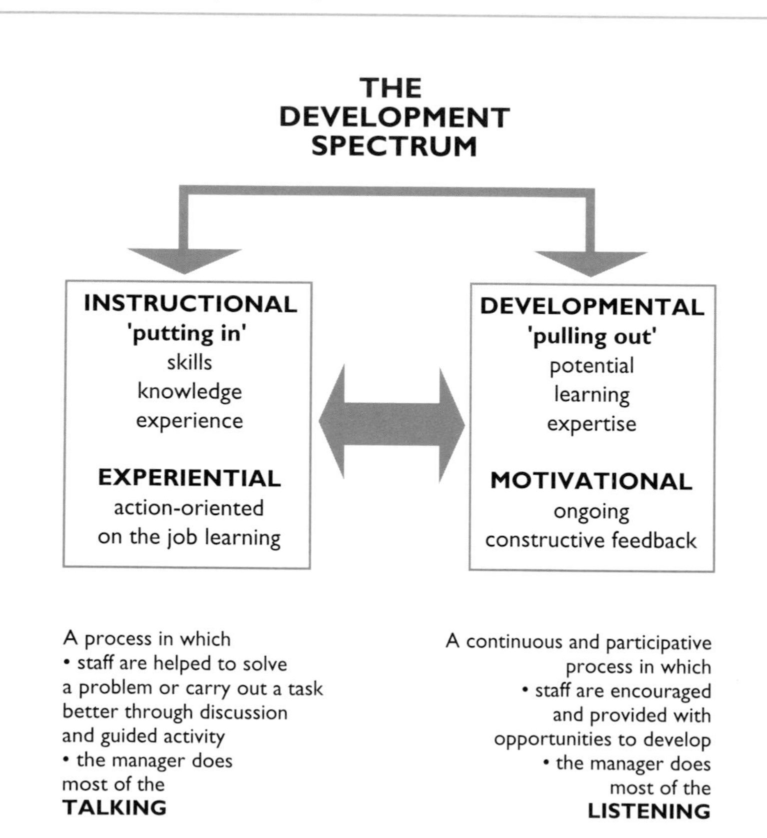

The practice development will challenge managers to find ways of getting close to their staff's practice and not base their assessment of practice solely on the staff's account of their own work. Social care governance will drive this agenda further.

Conclusion

In 1975 Bill Jordan addressed the BASW Annual Conference by challenging social workers to consider if they made decisions about their clients' lives as if they were 'fellow citizens' or as if their citizenship was somehow different to their own and in some way limited. The essence of his message was that social work should be a joint undertaking where information, decision-making and practice is a shared activity between clients and workers. Twenty-five years later these messages permeate not only social work rhetoric and literature but have also become enshrined in policies and legislation as professional practice continues to fall short of the ideals of partnership, empowerment and inclusion.

In many ways this study challenges organisations to consider whether they make plans and decisions about practice and service developments in partnership with their managers, staff and service users; or, are staff and service users' experiences somehow regarded as too subjective and therefore limited? The findings suggest that practice and service developments should be a joint undertaking between managers, staff and service users where information, decision-making and practice are shared activities and the ideals of partnership, empowerment and inclusion are integral to organisational culture and management practice.

It's a simple message – deceptively so – yet the danger is that it could remain an aspiration rather than a reality, as organisations look for quick fix solutions to the problems they face. If organisations really are serious about creating the conditions that encourage and support staff to adapt, change and develop how they work, they need to listen to, reflect on and learn from their experiences. Otherwise, management practices will continue to fall short of the ideals of partnership, empowerment and inclusion and the reservoir of information and intelligence of staff will remain untapped throughout the organisation. The reality is that this can only be achieved with persistent effort over time (Smale).

References

BASW (1980) *Clients are Fellow Citizens*, Birmingham: BASW

Carnall, C.A. (1990) *Managing Change in Organisations*, London: Prentice Hall

Covey, S.R. (1992) *The Seven Habits of Highly Effective People*, London, Simon & Schuster

Covey, S.R. (1996) *Principle-centred Leadership*, London: Simon & Schuster

Clutterbuck, D. (1992) *Mentoring*, Henley

DHSS (NI) (1990) *People First: Community Care in Northern Ireland in the 1990s*, Belfast: HMSO

Department of Health (1995) *Child Protection: Messages from Research*, London: DOH

Handy, C. (1994) *The Empty Raincoat*, Arrow Business Books

Holbeche, L. (1997) *Career Development, the Impact of Flatter Structures on Careers*, Butterworth Heinemann

Kalinauckas, P. and King, H. (1994) *Coaching: Realising the Potential*, IPD

Kanter, R. Moss, (1989) *When Giants Learn to Dance: Mastering the Challenges of Strategy, Management and Careers in the 1990s*, New York: Simon & Schuster

Kearney, P. (1996) *The Management of Practice Expertise Project*, London, NISW

Kirk, D. (1997) 'Loyalty: the High Price of Bottom-line Practices', based on research by Snaders and Sidney in the *Belfast Newsletter* (19 August)

Kolb, D. (1983) *Experiential Learning*, London: Prentice Hall

Mayo, A. and Lank, E. (1995) 'The Learning Organisation: From Vision to Action' in *People Management* (16 Nov)

Mumford, A. (1995) *Effective Learning*, Training Extras, IPD

Payne, M. (1994) 'Personal Supervision in Social Work' in Connor, A. and Stewart, B. (eds.) *Performance Review and Quality in Social Care*, London: Jessica Kingsley

Pearn, M., Honey, P. and Clutterbuck, D. (1995) 'Learning from the Good, the Bad and the Ugly Mistakes' in *People Management* (30 Nov)

Pottage, D. and Evans, M. (1996) *The Competent Workplace – the View from Within*, London: NISW

Senge, P.M. (1990) *The Fifth Discipline: The Art and Science of the Learning Organisation*, London: Century

Simmons, M. (1996) *New Leadership for Women and Men: Building an Inclusive Organisation*, Aldershot: Gower

Smale, G. (1996) *Mapping Innovation and Change*, London: HMSO

Smyth, C., Simmons, L. and Cunningham, G. (1999) *Quality Assurance in Social Work – a standards and audit approach for agencies and practitioners*, London: NISW

8 Developing practice learning: the practice teacher's perspective

George Wilson

Introduction

Practice teaching provision in Northern Ireland appears to enjoy significant advantages in comparison with other parts of the UK. The national survey by McCarthy and Walker (1994, p 1), for example, found that 'practice teachers based in Northern Ireland were more likely than those based elsewhere to be accredited and to be CCETSW award holders'. Since McCarthy and Walker's survey, the numbers of accredited practice teachers in Northern Ireland has further increased (81%) and agencies have continued to invest heavily in training with 66 per cent of practice teachers now award holders (CCETSW, 1997, p 6).

My experience as area placement co-ordinator for the Southern Health and Social Services Board (SH&SSB), however, has highlighted that my own agency has similar difficulties to others in Northern Ireland in terms of practice teacher turnover and meeting placement demand. The SH&SSB, like most other agencies, has invested heavily in training new practice teachers for the Award but, in spite of a considerable increase in qualified staff, the training team and freelance staff have continued to be overburdened in meeting placement quotas. My interest in undertaking this research arose from a desire to understand why, in spite of our apparent advantages in comparison with agencies in other parts of the UK, we were still experiencing these problems.

In Northern Ireland there has been little systematic study of practice teachers' perceptions of the problems outlined or analysis of their views and feelings about how they are managed, supported and trained. In carrying out this research with practice teachers in the SH&SSB (mainly singletons) I felt it was important to explore these issues from their perspective in the hope that innovative and creative ways of addressing problems would emerge. I also hoped that the knowledge and understanding acquired would help contribute to the wider academic and professional debate about the place of practice learning in social work education and training.

The chapter begins with a review of relevant literature and findings from previous research which influenced the focus of the study. The review includes a description of the organisational and policy context, followed by an overview of the specific agency context and an outline of the research methodology. I then analyse the main findings from the quantitative and qualitative data derived from practice teachers' responses to questionnaires and focus group interviews. The analysis identifies strengths and limitations of current arrangements for the management, support and training of practice teachers and explores issues such as turnover and lack of workload easement. Within this context a number of structural difficulties are highlighted associated with heavy reliance on the singleton model and the current policy of training new practice teachers to meet placement quotas. The final section considers the implications of these findings for the agency and other placement provider agencies that depend on the singleton model. A number of recommendations are proposed for developing practice learning, including the need for agencies to adopt a more strategic approach to the organisation of practice learning, incorporating a range of models for delivery, to develop further career opportunities within practice teaching, and to devise appropriate systems of support and reward to encourage the retention of experienced practice teachers.

The research context

From a comprehensive review of the literature Rogers (1996, p 3), concludes:

> carefully supervised practice is a fundamental, vital and indispensable component of social work education, and has been since its formulation as an academic discipline.

Indeed, comparative studies of social work education suggest that the value of practice learning appears to be recognised universally:

> Wherever in the world social work is practised, placements seem to be an essential part of social work courses (Doel and Shardlow, 1996, p 1).

Notwithstanding the importance attributed to practice learning, various writers have highlighted the rather ambiguous and insecure position practice teaching has occupied within social work education. Land (1996, p 25) has observed for example, that:

> from its inception in the 1970s until its gradual abolition in the 1990s the Certificate of Qualification in Social Work was haunted by an increasing deficiency in both the quantity and quality of placement opportunities for social work students.

Concomitant with the introduction of the new Diploma in Social Work (DipSW), the general aim of CCETSW's new policy of agency approval and practice teacher accreditation was designed to improve this situation and ensure the provision of high quality practice learning (CCETSW, 1992). Serious doubts remain however about the effectiveness of this policy in achieving these objectives. The study by Thompson and Marsh (1993, p 85) of a range of statutory and voluntary agencies in England and Wales perhaps encapsulates these continuing concerns:

> For too many agencies providing practice placements and practice teaching is seen as external, peripheral activities – as a no-cost exercise.

A number of studies have reported recurring problems in providing workload easement for practice teachers (Brodie, 1993; Karban, 1994). It has also been argued that endemic problems with easement have been exacerbated by increased demands on practice teachers resulting from the improved standards of the new DipSW requirements. In addition several writers have highlighted the increased stress experienced by practice teachers in carrying out their normal work generated by the major organisational and legislative changes during the 1990s (Mitchell, 1992; Balen *et al.*, 1993; Rogers, 1996).

Perhaps not surprisingly, given the range of problems outlined, studies throughout the UK have continued to report difficulties experienced by DipSW programmes in arranging good quality practice learning opportunities (McCarthy and Walker). Various studies have also highlighted recurring problems with practice teacher turnover and problems in retaining experienced staff. Karban, for example, reported that in Wakefield Social Services there was 'a loss of nearly two-thirds of all those practice teachers who have been accredited over the past three years'. As well as expressing concerns about quantity, Rickford (1996) worries about the threat to quality standards in DipSW training resulting from the decision by CCETSW in 1994 to abolish the requirement that practice teachers should be qualified social workers. Rickford's concern about quality standards appeared to be confirmed by CCETSW's national placement survey which found that:

> One in ten practice teachers was not qualified in social work, less than half were accredited by their agencies as practice teachers and only 26 per cent held CCETSW's Practice Teaching Award (McCarthy and Walker, p 1).

Mitchell (p 22) argues that a major underlying factor that has impeded the development of practice teaching envisaged in CCETSW's Paper 26.3 (1990) has been the overall lack of adequate government funding. While major concerns about the limitations of resources and organisational arrangements are recognised, comparatively little attention has been given to defining more precisely the optimal conditions and systems of support and reward which would facilitate practice teachers in delivering high-quality practice learning. Perhaps as a result of the difficulties of addressing these issues the strategy of many placement providers has been to deal with turnover problems by continuing to recruit and train greater numbers of new practice teachers. Karban (p 24), for example, concluded from the Wakefield survey that:

> without the recruitment of significant numbers of new practice teachers the department would be unable to meet its partnership commitments in terms of numbers of student placements.

Rogers, however, has observed that there have been few empirical studies of practice teachers' motivation for undertaking training or their perception of its adequacy in addressing their needs.

The Northern Ireland context

There is evidence to indicate that a progressive development in practice learning in Northern Ireland is affected by similar problems to those elsewhere in the UK. In marked contrast to the situation in many other parts of the UK, Northern Ireland has a high rate of accredited practice teachers (81%) and Award Holders (66%) (CCETSW, 1997). While these figures seem encouraging, the placement survey by Rea (1994, p 9) found that lack of workload easement and additional remuneration were major disincentives to practice teachers in Northern Ireland remaining in this role. Although there was no indication that any agencies had resorted to using non-social work qualified staff, Rea (p 9) also found high rates of practice teacher turnover, for example three of the four Area Boards had turnover rates of 50 per cent.

Agencies here have continued to invest heavily in the recruitment and training of new practice teachers in order to meet the increasing demand for placements resulting from increased recruitment to DipSW programmes; for example, in 1998–99, 314 placements were provided for university-based students. A recent survey of the twenty approved local agencies showed that 481 practice teachers held the award, with a further 61 in training (TOPSS, 1999, Appendix 1, Table 4). The findings of CCETSW's (1997) survey in Northern Ireland, which considered the problems of retaining practice teachers alongside an increased demand for placements, were similar to Karban's (p 24) study in concluding that, in order to meet placement demand, 'there will continue to be a need to train practice teachers annually'.

The research study

The research study was undertaken with practice teachers in the SH&SSB. This is a CCETSW-approved agency for practice learning and, since 1992 has had a purchaser–provider system for the delivery of practice learning opportunities with the four Trusts within the Board area. Overall management responsibility for social work training including practice teaching is held by a training consortium which includes directors of social services from each trust and representatives from the Board's training department. Operational management of practice learning is delegated to the area placement co-ordinator who works in conjunction with co-ordinators in each Trust (senior social services managers) to plan and agree placement availability, monitor and evaluate provision, and review practice teaching issues.

The annual placement quota for the SH&SSB (34) is established by the Department of Health and Social Services (DHSS NI). In addition, the agency provides placements for eight to ten employment-based students annually. When this study was conducted in 1998, there were 71 practice teachers in the SH&SSB. Apart from a small number of staff employed by the Board's social services training unit, most practice teachers in the area are singletons. Since 1991 an average of eight staff from the Board have been trained each year through the Northern Ireland Practice Teachers' Training Programme (NIPTTP) and hold the Practice Teacher's Award. The rest, all accredited by the agency, have been trained through short in-service courses and many of them hold the award via the portfolio route. Support for practice teachers is provided by a development group which meets on a regular basis (usually every two months). In addition to training sessions offered outside the agency the practice teachers' development group provides refresher training for staff. Support, guidance and advice is available to singleton practice teachers on request from members of the training unit in each Trust. The Board provides each Trust with funding to help and support practice teachers through, for example, workload easement. Trusts currently receive £2000 per placement, including an additional £200 traditionally provided by the SH&SSB to assist in developing practice learning. Each Trust is expected to provide a quota of placements agreed in a formal contract.

Methodology

The study focused on the themes of management, support and training of practice teachers. Research methods were chosen on the basis of their appropriateness in facilitating the exploration and evaluation of practice teachers' perceptions of these issues. A postal questionnaire was the primary instrument of data collection and was circulated to all 71 practice teachers in the SH&SSB. A total of 66 (93%) of questionnaires were returned. This high rate of return helps to validate the discussion of findings and also reflects the interest demonstrated by practice teachers. The questionnaire was pre-coded and structured in categories to facilitate analysis by the Statistical Package for the Social Services (SPSS, Version 7.5). A draft questionnaire was piloted with four practice teachers from a voluntary agency. This process proved invaluable and the questionnaire was modified in the light of feedback prior to circulation. These modifications included, for example, additional Likert scales designed to elicit levels of satisfaction with support and also perceptions about the status of practice teaching within the agency.

The questionnaire was designed to elicit quantitative data, including for example, the length of practice teacher experience and the number of students taken during particular years. Open-ended questions were included to gather more qualitative data and allow for fuller expression of views and feelings, such as what practice teachers enjoyed most and least about their role. To provide triangulation, two focus group meetings were held with practice teachers. One took place at the beginning of the research to inform the design of the study. The second was held following analysis of the questionnaire in order to facilitate interpretation of the results and add depth to the study. To further validate the data supplied by practice teachers, a focus group meeting was held with Trust placement co-ordinators. In addition, semi-structured interviews were carried out with four tutors responsible for placement co-ordination in each DipSW programme to help contextualise the study. All data entered on SPSS was checked to assure the quality of the material prior to analysis. Qualitative data from practice teacher questionnaires and from focus group meetings is referred to in the findings. The findings discussed below present a summarised version of a larger study (Wilson, 1998).

Findings and discussion

Practice teacher characteristics and motivation

The results indicated that 21 practice teachers (31.8%) were male and 45 (68.2%) female. Most practice teachers were either at senior social worker grade (28, 42.4%), or social work grade (24, 36.4%). A large majority (52, 78.8%) were from fieldwork settings. Echoing Land's (1996) concerns about the lack of residential and day-care placements in the north-east of England, only 2 (3%) in the SH&SSB worked in these settings. The majority (47, 71.2%) held a primary degree, and 16 (24.2%) held a masters qualification. It was found that a desire for personal professional development was ranked highest (26, 39.4%) among factors motivating staff to undertake the practice teaching role. The results also indicated that a majority of practice teachers intended to work towards obtaining the post-qualifying and advanced awards in social work, 39 (59.1%) and 41 (62.1%) respectively. Overall, these figures indicate that practice teachers in the SH&SSB are a well-qualified group with clear aspirations to continue their professional development and acquisition of qualifications. While these are positive findings they also have worrying implications for practice teachers being available for future placements.

Practice teacher training and learning needs

All practice teachers in the SH&SSB hold a social work qualification and are accredited by the agency. It was found that 55 (83.3%) hold the Practice Teachers' Award and that the majority (44, 66%) had been practice teaching for four years or longer. These results represent a significant improvement on McCarthy and Walker's survey and are also above the Northern Ireland average (CCETSW, 1997). A range of qualitative data emerged from the research indicating that the competence-based the NIPTTP was generally viewed positively by practice teachers:

> A positive experience which facilitated practice teaching skills, knowledge and confidence.

Practice teachers highlighted personal and professional learning as a result of the award course:

> I think the student benefited from me being on the course; there is no doubt about it, you gained in confidence and you had to stand back and look at your practice.

While they were positive about the adequacy of the award course in preparing them to undertake the role, a number of practice teachers expressed concern about the demands and stress of having to prove themselves competent with one student at the same time as managing their normal workload:

> I feel individuals need to be fully aware of the demands, stress and pressure.

> I found the course comprehensive and very demanding.

Award course practice teachers generally found their competence-based training more adequate than staff who had undertaken traditional short in-service courses. The evidence indicated, however, that some staff in the latter category had been able to make up for perceived deficiencies in their initial training by undertaking refresher training courses:

> I first started practice teaching prior to the introduction of the award – the short period of training was minimal – subsequent training did help me to address some of the key issues, e.g. anti-racist and anti-discriminatory practice, adult learning theory…

Regardless of the form of their initial training, the majority of practice teachers rated working with a failing student, assessment of competence, and coping with the stress of practice teaching among their most significant current learning needs. For some, particularly those who carried out this role less frequently, their needs in this area appeared to be connected with concerns and anxieties about standards in competence-based learning:

> I thought I was OK on assessment but took some time out and when I came back to practice teaching the competences had changed – I found it quite difficult to get used to the new jargon.

> Sometimes you have a student who is just meeting the competences and only just meeting them; but there is something just not right here, the student could easily go the other direction and it is trying to think, are we making it here or not.

Such concerns were also reflected in the significant numbers of staff (38, 59.4%) who were uncertain or dissatisfied with their ability to undertake the process of involving a second opinion practice teacher (still an option in Northern Ireland).

The study found that practice teachers were generally positive about working relationships with tutors. Concerns were expressed, however, by some singleton practice teachers about situations where there had been disagreement over assessment standards:

> You are at a great disadvantage – they are academics and they know the student – you only have them for this period.

> The least enjoyable part is getting on the same wavelength with tutors if and when difficulties are apparent.

Concerns about the power differential with tutors were not as evident in the responses from practice teachers employed by the training team who would normally take more students on a regular basis. Variations in responses could possibly be explained by factors including differences in practice teachers level of experience, frequency of contact with tutors, positions in the organisation and variations in level of support. These findings would suggest the need for further research to explore the relationship between practice teachers and tutors in order to investigate the impact of these variables more fully.

Management and support

The majority of singleton practice teachers (38, 60.3%) were either dissatisfied or very dissatisfied with the amount of workload easement they had received to carry out their role. The findings in relation to singletons are consistent with findings in other studies such as that by Williamson (1989) which reported that the 'most widespread and deeply rooted concern amongst [them] was the lack of time and space to do the job properly' (p 3). Perhaps not surprisingly, stress was identified by 30 staff (45.5%) as the least enjoyable aspect of practice teaching. Twenty-two staff (33.3%) identified writing the students' assessment report as a stress factor:

> The least enjoyable aspect of being a practice teacher is working at night at home to complete reports and coping with the stress of additional work.

> No workload easement – all reports were written at home – no time in lieu available.

There appeared to be a division of opinion among singleton practice teachers about the status of practice teaching within the agency. While a small majority, 37 (56.9%) rated the status medium-to-high, 24 (36.9%) felt it was low. Comments received in relation to this question suggested that practice teaching was generally perceived as valued and supported within social work teams and by other practice teachers, but less recognised or appreciated by more senior management:

> Status is medium-to-high in that the qualification is highly recognised but the actual practice is not given much status.

> Practice teaching is accorded high status among both colleagues and staff, but low priority with management who see it as diminishing my time as manager.

In a range of possible resources, 36 (54%) identified their line manager as the single most important source of support. Only 6 (9.1%) identified the tutor as an important source of support.

Another concern was that only 11 (16.7%) regularly attended the agency's development group that offers support and refresher training. While those who did attend meetings generally found them helpful, a significant number (34, 51.5%) reported that they had not attended refresher training since their initial training. Among the reasons given for non-attendance the following were typical comments:

> It is difficult to justify going if the team is under pressure.

Some singletons appeared to feel that they only had practice teaching status when they were actively taking students:

> I would only go if I had a student on placement and even then I am often too busy.

In spite of concerns about lack of support and status within the organisation it was clear from the findings that most singletons continued to find the experience and challenge of working with students rewarding. For most practice teachers (44, 66%) seeing students progress in their learning and development was the most enjoyable aspect of the work:

> It is very satisfying to see a student developing professionally and growing in confidence.

Twenty-one practice teachers (31.8%) also highlighted their satisfaction with the opportunity provided to develop their own practice:

> It is a challenge that allowed me to examine my own role, work and attitudes more clearly.

> It is interesting, stimulating and challenging work and helps me as a team leader engaged in social work.

Practice teacher availability and aspirations

The findings indicated that the most common pattern among singletons was to take one student every other year with some taking a break of two years or longer. Inadequate workload easement was reported as the most common reason why they had not taken a student during the period 1993–98. However, the findings also showed a wide range of other structural factors in the agency that may account for the shortage of practice teachers (see Figure 8.1).

While the findings indicated differing perceptions about whether possession of the Practice Teachers' Award had actually enhanced career prospects, it was evident that significant numbers of staff had gained promotion (12, 18.2%) or changed job role (17, 25.8%). Taken together with the earlier findings concerning aspirations to complete post-qualifying or advanced awards these results confirm the view that practice teachers generally are a mobile group of staff who tend to use opportunities for obtaining additional professional qualifications or career development.

Figure 8.1 Reasons for not taking students

Reasons for not taking students (1993–98)	No. giving this as a reason	%
Lack of workload easement	18	27.3
Change of job role	17	25.8
Lack of financial remuneration	14	21.2
Need to take a break between students	12	18.2
Promotion	12	18.2
Undertaking further training	9	13.6
Organisational changes in workplace	9	13.6
Maternity leave	8	12.1

The large majority of staff nevertheless confirmed their intention to continue as practice teachers during the next five years with only 6 (9.5%) stating they would discontinue involvement and 7 (10.6%) unsure. Although these results seem encouraging, the variety of reasons given by singletons for not taking students, along with their desire for further professional qualifications and career enhancement, suggest that availability is affected by factors that are not always predictable by either the agency or the practice teacher. It would be reasonable to assume that such factors, often occurring at short notice and familiar to all those involved in placement co-ordination, are particularly acute for agencies like the SH&SSB which rely heavily on singletons rather than staff in training departments where practice teaching is an integral part of the job. This background of structural instability and anticipated future uncertainty makes it difficult to predict practice teacher availability and therefore makes rational placement planning problematic for agencies such as the SH&SSB.

Sustaining commitment to practice teaching: possible incentives

Practice teachers were asked in a multiple-choice question to identify the most important incentives which would encourage them to continue to take students. Financial remuneration was identified as the most important incentive by 56 (84.8%), and 53 (80.3%) identified workload easement. While it was clear that some were prepared to take students without workload easement as long as they received financial remuneration, most preferred a combination of these two incentives:

> I don't believe that staff will really see practice teaching as worthwhile until they are at least recognised via some payment.

> Introduce some financial recompense and insist on workload easement.

Significantly, while adequate workload easement was seen as a desirable incentive and one which had clearly worked effectively in some areas, a number of practice teachers, particularly team leaders, were sceptical about whether it could be achieved:

> It is barely possible as a team leader to get the type of easement that is appropriate to meet managerial responsibilities.

> Our Trust always lets us know money is available but it is not always possible to arrange easement.

Although they ranked it lower than financial remuneration and workload easement, significant numbers of singletons expressed interest in either specialist part-time (36, 54.5%) or full-time practice teaching posts (20, 30.3%). In relation to the interest in a part-time post it was evident that some would value opportunities to remain in practice while having adequate time and space to undertake practice teaching:

> The idea of developing a specialist practice teaching role – alongside a small and protected caseload – may go towards prioritising this role and give it a higher profile in the agency.

Conclusions and recommendations

This study of practice teachers in the SH&SSB identified both strengths in agency provision and areas requiring further development. While these findings are pertinent to the Board they would also seem to have implications for developing practice learning in other agencies, particularly those which also depend heavily on singleton models.

The findings indicated that the SH&SSB have a highly qualified group of practice teachers, the large majority of whom are award holders. If practice teaching qualifications are taken as the basic quality standard then it would be possible to conclude that the SH&SSB, in common with most other agencies in Northern Ireland, has significant advantages over other parts of the UK. The findings of this research suggest, however, that qualifications by themselves do not guarantee that practice teachers will feel confident and supported in carrying out their role. The lack of confidence reported by many singletons in assessing competence and working with the failing student is clearly a cause for concern. Evidence was found in this study that some practice teachers were able to make up for deficits in initial training through refresher training and gaining further experience. The finding that many singletons did not attend refresher training and did not take students every year also gives cause for concern.

An assumption underpinning Paper 26.3, which aimed to improve the quality of practice learning, was that practice teachers would continue to gain experience in this role and usually offer more than one placement annually. However, the findings of this research indicate that practitioners and managers are now so preoccupied in carrying out their normal work that practice teaching on a regular basis envisaged by Paper 26.3 presents an extremely difficult challenge. Compounding these difficulties, as Rogers (1996) has observed, is the fact that practice teaching with the new DipSW now demands 'a more structured time consuming and demanding involvement' (p 19). The finding in this study that many practice teachers were also dissatisfied with the support they had received from the agency, including a lack of workload easement, amounts to a positive disincentive to taking on a role perceived by many to be stressful and demanding.

Inadequacies of current strategy

The results of this study support Land's (1996) findings, which indicated that problems with practice teacher availability are not simply caused by inadequate workload easement. A range of reasons was given for not taking students, confirming that complex structural factors impacting on social work agencies and social workers were continuing to affect availability. This suggests that devising more effective methods of workload easement, put forward as a principal solution to this problem, would not by itself be a panacea (Rea, 1994).

Ironically, findings from the current study suggested that the successful introduction of CCETSW's post-qualifying framework in Northern Ireland (Darragh, 1996) may have impeded the retention of experienced practice teachers. Although practice teachers were found to be a highly motivated and well-qualified group, many singletons were frequently unavailable to the agency for extended periods while they pursued further qualifications. It is also of significance that a substantial number of practice teachers in this study indicated an interest in achieving the Advanced Award. Given that practice teaching is positioned at post-qualifying level, the desire to gain advanced credits inevitably means that staff will be unavailable to act as practice teachers while they pursue other work to demonstrate advanced competence.

Significantly, a majority of practice teachers in the SH&SSB are at senior social worker/team leader grade. Characteristically it has been this group of staff who have been expected by their agencies to play a key role in implementing the various organisational, policy and legislative changes that have impacted on the agency in recent years, further limiting their availability. While there were mixed feelings about the value of the Practice Teacher Award, the findings showed that significant numbers had either changed job roles or obtained promotion since gaining the qualification. It would seem that practice teaching for a considerable number of staff may lead to career enhancement within the agency but limit their availability as practice teachers. Collectively, these factors raise doubts about the validity of the agency's current strategy of relying heavily on singletons and continuing to train new practice teachers to meet placement quotas. The findings suggest that this approach has not been able to guarantee a quota of placements.

Some singleton practice teachers have also raised issues about quality highlighting, for example, a lack of confidence in assessing students' performance in situations where they have not been able to take students on a regular basis. Although no guarantee of quality, it is reasonable to assume that taking students on a regular basis is necessary to acquire and sustain the competence required to carry out this role effectively. Consequently, the agency's current strategy, which may have been effective initially, no longer seems adequate in working environments that are now more complex and stressful, and where there is greater demand for placements and higher DipSW standards to meet.

A comprehensive strategy for developing practice learning

The findings suggest that there is a need in the SH&SSB to devise a more comprehensive strategy for developing practice learning. While the findings raise concerns about the agency's current heavy reliance on the singleton model, the results also suggest that the solution would not be to abandon this approach entirely. As indicated in the research, singletons are a highly qualified group with considerable expertise to offer DipSW students, and most confirmed their desire to continue in practice teaching. A fundamental element of the agency's strategy therefore should be aimed at creating the organisational conditions in which singletons feel valued, supported and adequately rewarded to carry out the role on a regular basis in order to sustain quality of performance.

At the same time it is clear from the findings that over-reliance on singletons is likely to continue to present problems for the agency in meeting placement quotas. Consequently, another key ingredient of a comprehensive strategy should be directed at reducing this overdependence by establishing a greater range of models for delivering practice learning. Based on the findings a strong case can be made for the creation of new specialist part-time or full-time practice training posts. The development of such posts at senior practitioner grade would provide the benefit to staff of having a career structure within practice teaching. The findings indicated that this development would be welcomed by many practice teachers in the SH&SSB and creating such posts would also benefit the agency since even part-time practice teachers would be expected to take several students per year. New placement sites, including those in residential and day-care settings, could be developed to diversify the range and increase availability.

The following were among the principal recommendations for improving the infrastructure of practice teaching in the SH&SSB. They may also be applicable to other agencies seeking to devise a more comprehensive strategy for developing practice learning.

1 The agency should consider creating part-time and/or full-time practice teacher posts at senior practitioner grade.
2 The agency should consider payment of financial remuneration to singleton practice teachers as part of a contractual arrangement to provide placements on a regular basis.
3 Consideration should be given by the agency to reviewing current systems for financing workload easement in order to develop more effective and uniform approaches across all Trusts.
4 Consideration should be given to recruiting more singleton practice teachers and developing more placement sites in residential and day-care.
5 Trust management should encourage and facilitate practice teachers' attendance at development group meetings and refresher training.
6 In order to enhance the qualification and status of practice teaching CCETSW should consider introducing a Practice Teacher Award at Advanced Level.

Implementing these recommendations for improving organisational structures, support mechanisms and incentives for practice teachers would have significant financial and resource implications for the agency. (The proposal to establish the Practice Teachers Award at Advanced Level would also require a policy shift by CCETSW that would have considerable implications not least for current award holders). Nevertheless, it is argued that these changes are essential in order to enhance the status of practice teachers and provide a more solid organisational and professional foundation for the future development of practice learning.

On the basis of this research there is evidence to indicate that the current use of financial resources for practice teaching is not cost-effective or efficient.

Indeed it can be argued that our present system for the delivery of practice teaching carries with it additional, often hidden costs, particularly in the areas of practice teacher turnover and placement breakdown. Implementing these proposals would undoubtedly require some additional funding, although this could be minimal as savings could be made from better use of existing resources, for example the need for less expenditure on practice teacher training.

The main conclusion of this study is that agencies must find better ways of supporting and rewarding practice teachers to carry out an increasingly complex and demanding role. The research demonstrates that listening to practice teachers and developing a greater understanding of their needs can help agencies in this task and assist them in developing high-quality practice learning. If agencies become more responsive in meeting practice teachers' needs they will be more able to meet the needs of their students, the demands of their employers and ultimately the service needs of clients (Rogers, 1996).

References

Balen, R., Brown, K. and Taylor, C. (1993) ' "It seems so much is expected of us": Practice Teachers, the Diploma in Social Work and Anti-Discriminatory Practice', *Social Work Education*, Vol. 12, No. 3

Brodie, I. (1993) 'Teaching from Practice in Social Work Education: A study of the Content of Supervision Sessions', *Issues in Social Work Education*, Vol. 13, Pt 2

CCETSW (NI) (1997) *Review of the Northern Ireland Practice Teacher Training Programme 1990–1996*, unpublished report to DHSS Inspectorate.

CCETSW (1992) *Guidance on Approval of Agencies Providing Practice Learning Opportunities*, Paper 26.3, London: Central Council for Education and Training in Social Work

Darragh, E. (1996) 'Post Qualifying Awards for Social Workers'. *Child Care in Practice*, Vol. 3, Pt 2

Doel, M. and Shardlow, S. (1996) *Social Work in a Changing World: An International Perspective on Practice Learning*, Aldershot: Ashgate

Karban, K. (1994) 'Where's Teacher?' *Community Care*, 8–14

Land, J. (1996) 'Practice Learning – a lack of opportunities', *Practice*, Vol. 8, No. 2

McCarthy, P. and Walker, J. (1994) *CCETSW: UK Audit of Practice Placements 1992–93*, University of Newcastle

Mitchell, D. (1992) 'Practice What You Teach', *Community Care*

Rea, E. (1994) *Practice Placements Study*, London: DHSS

Rickford, F. (1996) 'Practice Makes Perfect', *Community Care* 10–16

Rogers, G. (1996) 'The Voices of Practice Teachers in Britain and Canada: Comparing Views After Training', *Issues in Social Work Education*, Vol. 16, Pt 1

Thompson, S. and Marsh P. (1993) 'A Little Out of Place', *Community Care*

TOPSS (1999) *A First Class Service*, consultation document, Training Organisation for the Personal Social Services Northern Ireland

Williamson, H. (1989) *Assessment of Practice: A Perennial Concern?* Cardiff: School of Social and Administrative Studies, University of Wales

Wilson, G. (1998) *A Critical Examination of Practice Teaching Provision in the Southern Health and Social Services Board*, MSc Advanced Social Work Thesis (unpublished), Belfast: QUB/UU